Modern Magic

MANTRAS FOR DAILY LIFE

Modern Magic
MANTRAS FOR DAILY LIFE

KIRSTEN RIDDLE

FINDHORN PRESS

Published in 2012 by Findhorn Press, Scotland

ISBN 978-1-84409-598-8

Edited by Jacqui Lewis
Cover design and illustrations by Richard Crookes
Interior design by Damian Keenan
Printed and bound in the EU

1 2 3 4 5 6 7 8 9 17 16 15 14 13 12

Published by
Findhorn Press
117-121 High Street,
Forres IV36 1AB,
Scotland, UK

t +44 (0)1309 690582
f +44 (0)131 777 2711
e info@findhornpress.com
www.findhornpress.com

Dedication

This book is dedicated to all the wise
and powerful women in my life,
who use a little modern magic every day
even if they don't realize it!

My mum for her love.
*
My gran for her spirit.
*

*My Auntie Dot for her strength
and never-ending belief
in the power of magic!*

Acknowledgements

I'd like to acknowledge the help and
support of the following people:

Sabine Weeke,
Jacqui Lewis,
Mary Bryce (CHAT - IT'S FATE),
Katy Evans (SOUL & SPIRIT),
Golnaz (SOUL & SPIRIT)

Contents

Contents

Foreword

I have always believed in magic. But then I have always had a vivid imagination. As a child, I remember climbing under my bedclothes, closing my eyes, and believing that I could fly. That the bed would take me off on some fantastic adventure whilst I slept. And of course it did, through the land of dreams, which we now know is governed by the subconscious mind. When I closed a book the story didn't end there. In my head it continued, and often with me as the central character. This creativity has helped me look at things in new and exciting ways and it's this ability to perceive things differently that is the key to magic.

I became interested in the tarot at the age of sixteen. The images struck a chord with me, and I remember investing in my first pack of cards, and spending hours leafing through them, taking each picture and stepping into it in my mind. I found it easy to connect with them, and tell a story through the pattern of the cards. To me, giving a reading is like opening a book. You let the pages fall upon a chapter in your life, and let the powerful images do the rest. From there I started reading professionally. I travelled around the UK and attended some of the biggest Mind, Body, Soul conventions. Being only eighteen, I was probably one of the youngest readers, but that didn't stop me. I had a thirst for knowledge, and I felt at home in the spiritual arena. I learnt about the power of meditation, and the ability to visualize, which isn't hard when you're a natural daydreamer!

I attended sessions, and I delivered them too. I discovered the magic in stretching your comfort zone, and to this day I believe in setting personal challenges, and being spontaneous once in a while. It's medicine for the soul.

For me the transition from a psychic to a magical practitioner was a natural one. Magic relies on intuition to flourish. It needs energy and focus, and the ability to be creative. Most of all, it asks us to return to our childhood, not in whimsical fancy, but in the way we look at the world. This planet is a beautiful place, a fascinating, mesmerizing, curious space. It's about the way we see it. Do we look through jaded eyes, or do we open them a little wider? Do we use our minds, and utilize the power of thought, or do we continue to see in black and white? The answer is clear to me. We can make our world a better place. We can transform our lives and manifest the things we want. We can help others see and appreciate the magic. And most importantly we can inject some fun and enchantment into every day. This is why I have written this book. If nothing else, I hope it gives you something to think about. Because our thoughts are nuggets of power, sprinkles of stardust that can change the world.

Introduction

IMAGINE IF YOU CAN a long and winding road. A weary traveller makes his way down this road, his head held low, his shoulders hunched. As he plods on he notices an old man sitting nearby. He shouts, "Old man, old man, pray tell me, what are the people like in the next village?"

The old man looks amused. He asks, "What were the people like in the last village?"

The traveller grimaces, "They were miserable. They didn't make me feel welcome at all."

The old man smiles, and replies, "Well, I expect they'll be much the same in the next village."

The traveller agrees, pulls a face and continues on his path. An hour or so passes and soon he stumbles across the next village. Just as he expects, the villagers are unfriendly, they don't smile and they don't make him feel welcome.

A little time passes and another traveller is walking down the very same road. He walks with his head held high, face to the sun, smiling. He too spots the old man sitting there minding his own business. The traveller shouts a cheery hello, and then asks, "Pray tell me, what are the people like in the next village?"

The old man replies, "Say, what were they like in the last village?"

The traveller smiles and says, "Oh they were delightful, so friendly. They really made me feel welcome."

The old man also smiles, and replies, "Well then, I expect they will be the same in the next village," to which the traveller agrees. Soon he comes across the next village and just as he expects the villagers are warm, friendly and very welcoming.

The moral of this tale is obvious: you get what you expect. If you have a positive outlook, then you will see things in a positive light. If you are negative, then everything is weighed down by a huge cloud of dark energy. The mind is a powerful tool that affects everyone's experience of life. If the way we think has such a powerful effect on us in the present, then it makes sense that it should also be able to shape our future. The mind creates our thoughts, which appear as pockets of energy that we send out to the universe. It's a magical tool and, if used in the right way – with focus, positive intent and energy – it can manifest the things we want, and enhance our world. This is the essence of mind magic and what this book is all about.

Let's think for a minute about traditional magic. It works using the following principles: focus, intention, energy and ritual. The ritual is the final step; it's the part of the magic that becomes or 'fixes' the spell, for example the herbal mix, or the candle magic. This step is important because it helps us to focus our energy and produce something to match our intent. We use ingredients that link to our aim and reinforce our mission. However, we can still perform magic without this element – we just need to find a new way of focusing intentions. So rather than investing in ingredients that we are unsure of, we can use our mind to fix the magic with a visualization or a mantra. We can use an everyday ritual, something that's easy to do as we get ready for work, or have our breakfast, to secure the same outcome. All we have to do is change our perception of what we are doing. In other words, we have to learn to see the magic in the everyday and make it work for us. Simple things like the words we use or the stories we tell ourselves become incredibly powerful magical tools if used in the right way.

This book shows you how to do this. It introduces you to the power of your mind, the latent energy within, and how you can use this for self-development and empowerment. Just by thinking differently, you can change your world in a positive way. This book shows you the importance of creativity and how to stretch the imagination muscle. It illustrates the magic inherent in every day and shows you how to shift perception and enchant your life.

Mantras and Rituals

The mantras and rituals that you will find in this book have been created with modern living in mind. They're based on everyday routines; things that may seem mundane on first look, but with a little bit of magical intent can be used to enhance your world. They are created to make the most of busy lifestyles and make the brain work a little harder. In other words, you don't need special ingredients or settings to make the magic work, because you have everything you need in your head or at your fingertips.

The word "mantra" comes from the Sanskrit and means a tool or instrument of thought. A mantra can be a repeated word or phrase, a picture, or a visualization. It doesn't matter exactly what form it takes; the key is in the change that it creates. A mantra can help you to perceive things differently by developing new thought patterns.

Mind mantras are your secret weapon. They can be done anywhere, at any time, and because you say or visualize them silently, no one need be any the wiser. There is no grand gesture, no need to chant, or intone spells (although if you do want to go down that route then that's fine too). Mind mantras work by using the power and energy of thought. This means that you can take our magic on the move and adapt it to your busy schedule.

Ritual is a part of life. Everything you do forms the basis of a ritual, from the moment you get up at an allotted time, to the moment you go to bed. How you brush your teeth is a ritual: do you start at one particular side? Do you wet the toothbrush first, or take a sip of water? These might seem like insignificant things, but everyone has a way of doing them that has been developed over the years. We put them together in a certain order that becomes habit.

Most rituals can be adapted for magical work. It's all about the way you see things. If you see brushing your teeth as a simple action to clean the mouth, remove plaque and create fresh breath, then that's great. But you might also choose to see it as a tool for cleansing to prepare you for the day ahead. As you clean and rinse, you rinse away any negative residue. You are refreshing your mouth so that you can speak clearly and with confidence throughout the day. Once you've finished you might want to make a magical statement to put you in the right frame of mind, for example "I am refreshed, clear-headed, and ready to communicate my desires to the world!"

Mix It Up

There is no set way to read this book – just dip in and see what you find. Read it from start to finish, or pick out the bits that interest you. If a suggestion doesn't appeal, no problem. You don't have to agree or connect with everything that's said in these pages. The beauty of mind magic is that you make your own way and develop a pattern of doing things that suits you. This book is a gentle guide, a tool to open doors and inspire you. At the end of the day you know your mind better than anyone else, so you know what is going to work for you. Enjoy experimenting and get creative. Your unique creative energy is what makes you who you are, and it's what gives you power. So start now. Take a deep breath. Picture yourself reading this book, being surprised and inspired. See the magic oozing from your pores. See yourself achieving great things. Know that this is the start of an exciting future. Smile and turn the page…

CHAPTER 1

Powerful Preparations

Before you start your magical journey there are a few things that need to be put in place. Imagine for a moment that you are a car. For that car to work effectively everything needs to be in good working order. There's no point even trying to get from A to B if you know that the brakes are rusty, or there's a problem with the clutch. Even small issues like loose screws or a broken stereo will mean that the journey won't be so pleasurable. This is why we put our cars through MOTs, get them checked regularly and keep on top of any issues. It's not always the same for our bodies, though.

We tend to forget that as humans we have a mind, a body and a soul, all of which are equally important and interrelated, and sometimes neglect one or other area. So perhaps you might feel OK physically, but emotionally drained. You might think you're on top of everything, but you keep getting that nagging pain in your lower back. It doesn't matter which part of our make-up we ignore; at the end of the day if we want to be firing on all cylinders, then we need to ensure that we are fit and well in mind, body, and soul. And if we want to use the vehicle of our being effectively, and for it to be able to take us to a magical destination where our dreams come true, then we need to prepare it for the journey.

Mind

The mind is like a computer: it directs and controls everything we do. Because of this, it must be first on the list for an MOT. Start by asking yourself how you feel at this moment in time. Be honest. If you could use one word to describe the state of your mind, what would it be?

The problem that most people face on a daily basis is too much information. We're bombarded with details and our minds are overloaded, which can cause stress, panic and a general feeling of not being able to cope. It's important to allow space for your thoughts to grow and for solutions to present themselves.

EXERCISE **Clear the clutter**

If you want to free your mind, try this simple visualization. Imagine for a moment that your mind is a large white room. Currently the room is filled with boxes of all different shapes and sizes. Each box is full of different things, from ideas yet to come to fruition to worries and problems. If this were a room in an actual house, we could easily set about clearing it up, so adopt the same approach and imagine how it will be to clear out the room that is your brain.

Find the biggest box of problems, and start to put all the smaller boxes containing worries and stresses inside, until all you have is one big, very full, box and lots of space. Next look at whatever boxes are left. Because you've tidied away your worries and problems, these should all be boxes of ideas and solutions. One by one, drop each of these boxes into the large box of problems. As you do so, picture the big box slowly reducing in size, until eventually it's a tiny box that you can hold in your hand. The ideas and solutions that you have provided have dissolved your worries. Put the box in your pocket and take a moment to embrace the emptiness of the room. Say "My mind is free, it is in tip-top condition and working for me."

TOP TIP

Make a mind tonic using fresh rosemary steeped in boiling water. Strain the liquid and add a spoonful of honey and a squeeze of lemon juice. Drink first thing in the morning for motivation and clarity.

Body

We all know the rules to help us maintain a healthy body. Eat plenty of fresh fruit and vegetables, get some exercise, plenty of sleep, and keep hydrated. These are simple things that we can and should make a part of our lifestyle. But from the point of view of this book there are additional things that we can do to make our body work better for us.

Flexibility is important; the more physically flexible we are, the more freely energy can circulate round the body and the more adaptable and able to go with the magical flow we can be.

EXERCISE Reach for the stars

Stand with your feet hip-width apart and your shoulders back and relaxed. Tilt your chin upwards. Imagine that you're going to try to reach the stars – obviously that's not physically possible, just imagine if it did happen! Stretch your arms and hands up. Feel the gentle pull up your spine and across your shoulders. Now rise slightly up on the balls of your feet and feel the stretch down your calves and up your thighs. As you do this, imagine a cord of gold tugging at the top of your head, pulling you even further up towards the universe. Picture energy flowing freely around your body. Now imagine grasping, with both hands, a star. Release it, slowly let your feet drop to the floor, bring your arms down and breathe deeply.

This a great exercise to do first thing in the morning as it raises energy levels and motivation.

TOP TIP

Pamper yourself every day, whether that means indulging in a candlelit meal, a luxurious bubble bath, or a little chocolate. It's good to treat your body. It does so much for you that it's only right that you should indulge your physical being and your senses a little.

Soul

Along with the mind and body, there is a spark of life that gives us the impetus to rise every day and to live. Without this inner fire or spirit, we'd be vacuous shells, wandering around leading a passionless life. We need this spirit – or soul, as you can think of it whatever your religious faith or other beliefs – to inspire us, to steer us to our destiny. Often the soul gets ignored. We're so busy focusing on the mind and body that we forget that we have this core spirit that can help us achieve great things. Every day, make a point of acknowledging your soul. Give thanks for its presence, because essentially it's what makes you human.

EXERCISE Russian dolls

Imagine for a moment that you are one of those Russian dolls, the type that live within each other. Your body is the outer doll, your mind is the one just inside and finally your spirit or soul is the innermost doll. Draw your attention back from your eyes so that it seems that you're looking out from deep inside your head, and then further back still, until you feel as if you are peering out of a house that is your body. This is your spirit energy. This is the core where everything you do comes from. Sit in this space and survey the world. Feel how removed you are from everyday stress and strain. Feel the energy like a flickering flame firing you up for action. Let any thoughts or impressions come to you in this space, any ideas or feelings that might urge you towards a course of action, or fulfilling a dream. Return to this space when you need guidance, or to retreat from the world and restore your energy. This is your spiritual haven, the home of your soul.

TOP TIP

Feed the soul with knowledge. Make a point of reading a new book every week or month, and don't just stick to the tried and tested. Choose something different, so if you normally go for fiction, try something factual instead. If you're normally into world history, then learn about plants and animals, or cooking. Don't limit yourself. The soul needs information to direct and inspire you.

~ Cleansing and Protection Techniques ~

In traditional magic it's recommended that you cleanse and protect yourself before casting spells. This is because magic is about raising energy, and some practices can make the connection to the spirit world stronger. Although this is nothing to be frightened of, it is a good idea to put some protection in place. In a way it's like leaving the door of your house open or ajar. Most people would ignore it, some friendly souls might endeavour to say hello, but there is the slight chance that someone harmful might see this as a chance to intrude into your home. So it's a case of being practical and remembering to turn the lock. If you leave the door open, you're also likely to leak precious energy. Think about your home. You wouldn't leave all the doors and windows open so that the heat could escape, would you? This is the same principle.

If you prepare yourself, and cleanse your aura thoroughly, your energy will be light and positive and more likely to attract spirits or beings with the same energy pattern. In other words, it's not a good idea to practise any kind of magic when you feel low, emotional or angry, because you'll be sending out negative

vibes to the universe and you're likely to attract the same kind of energy back.

Although mind magic doesn't tend to use spells in the traditional sense, you are still using the same formula of intention, energy and ritual, so it's a good idea to use preparation methods from traditional magic. Here are a few of the best techniques!

~ The Psychic Egg ~

In most cultures the egg is revered, and thought of as a symbol of rebirth and protection. In some cultures the egg was used to draw negative energy from the body and soul. Many magical traditions believe that if you roll an egg lightly over your body while imagining that it is cleansing you from the inside out, it will actually have this effect. When you have finished you should smash the egg, gather up the broken bits and place them in the rubbish while making a positive statement along the lines of "I release all negative energy to be transformed by light and love."

If you prefer something less physical (and messy!), you can use the image of the egg to protect your aura instead. Imagine that you are cocooned in an egg-like shell of golden light. This shell is super-powerful and can repel negative energy while keeping you safe and secure inside. You can do this at any time – perhaps when you feel under threat, or if you need to raise your energy levels. You can also cocoon other people in the shell, or place a huge golden egg over your entire home. The image itself is flexible, so play around with it.

~ Smudge Sticks ~

This is a technique used by the Native Americans. They perform this ritual before any spirit or dream work and it's also a powerful aid to healing. Traditionally they use bundles of dried sage, tied together and burned to create a scented smoke. They then waft this smoke around the body, cleansing every inch of the aura, the invisible energy field that surrounds the physical body. Many magical and esoteric retailers sell smudge sticks, but you can make up your own smudging tool, which is just as effective. You will need a handful of dried sage, and a bundle of feathers, roughly the same size as each other. Tie the feathers together so that you have a cluster that you can waft like a feather brush. Place the sage in a fireproof bowl and light, then waft the scented smoke around your body starting at the top of your head and working down either side. As you do this, visualize the smoke cleansing your aura of any negative energy, and see it shining brightly.

An alternative to burning dried sage is to gather fresh sage and steep it in boiling water. Place in a bowl and waft the vapours around your body. To increase the potency of this concoction you can add a squeeze of fresh lemon, a sprig of rosemary for strength and clarity, and/or a couple of drops of frankincense essential oil to help rejuvenate the spirit.

Once you have cleansed your aura, repeat the process and carry the bowl of scented liquid around the room, wafting the vapours from floor to ceiling and in every corner. This is a great ritual to perform when you move house, as it clears any stagnant energy and encourages a fresh, welcoming atmosphere.

It's not always easy or appropriate to carry out smudging when you're away from home or travelling, but there are alternatives that you can use. You could make up some sage water by steeping fresh sage in boiling water, straining and adding a sprinkling of lemon juice and a couple of drops of frankincense oil. Decant it into a bottle that you can carry with you. To give your mind magic a boost, just splash the water onto your wrists and massage in a circular motion. As you do this, visualize your entire body being cleansed and refreshed.

A sprig of fresh rosemary is also a handy tool to carry with you. In some folklore it's believed that rosemary bushes only grow in the presence of a powerful woman. They also signify clarity, mental aptitude and strength. You can keep a sprig in your pocket as a charm; just give it a squeeze before you perform any mantras or visualizations to help improve your focus.

Another great idea is to use everyday items that you may well already have about your person to help set you up for mind magic. So to focus your mind, and give yourself a boost, keep a compact mirror in your bag or pocket. Before any visualization or mantra, flick it open and spend a minute gazing at your reflection. Imagine the light from the mirror connecting with your eyes, stimulating your brain and clearing your head. Look into your eyes and imagine you are sending a message that bounces back and forth between you and your reflection. You can think something like, "I am powerful, I am effective, I make things happen." Continues repeating the mantra in a loop to give you strength and focus. You can use this technique at any time that you need a confidence boost, and you can change the statement to suit your needs. For example, if you've got a hot date, then you might say, "I am beautiful and lovable." Or if you have an important meeting at work you might say, "I am successful and eloquent. Everything I touch turns to gold."

The idea of a magical elixir has featured in folklore for centuries. It's a lovely thought – that finding and drinking the right concoction can give you magical powers and enhance your life. There might not be a fountain of youth at the end of your garden, or even an enchanting brew that can do this, but there are certain foods and drinks that, when combined, can give you an energy boost and improve your personal power.

For a personal power drink to cleanse body and soul, blend together a handful of ice, some chopped mango, several raspberries, and a squeeze of lemon. Serve in a tall glass with a sprig of mint.

If you prefer something warming, boil some water, pour in a cup, add a spoonful of honey, a spoonful of cider vinegar and a squeeze of lemon. This drink will have the same effect, and is a great pick-me-up in the mornings.

Experiment with different mixes of fruit to make your own power punch. All fruits have positive benefits, so do a bit of research and find out what makes you feel good inside and out. Generally speaking, warm liquids soothe and chilled liquids provide a cleansing boost. To increase the effect of the drink, visualize it travelling around your system as you drink, flowing around your body like a liquid stream of healing light.

Imagine you've been hit by a bolt of electricity. In reality it wouldn't be very pleasant but in magical terms it could be just what you need to cleanse your aura and prepare for magical work. Sit somewhere comfortable and close your eyes. Visualize a bolt of white lightning zigzagging its way down from the sky until it hits the centre of your scalp. Feel the power of the force zapping you with a blast of super energy. Feel the light buzzing around your aura, encasing your skin in a bright white glow. The force of the lightning pushes everything dark or stagnant out of your aura, where it dissolves into the ether.

Now imagine you have a thermostat situated just below your chest and above your belly-button. This small dial controls the brightness of your aura and increases your power. Picture yourself turning the dial up. As you do so, your aura gets brighter and thicker.

This effective technique, which I call the Aura Sweep, can help when you need to attract attention, or give your confidence a boost.

As well as improving your personal power, you can use your aura as a 'lasso' to draw people into your world. Just imagine it extending outwards in a large loop, so that people get caught in the circle of light. See them standing in the glow of your aura, and smile.

~ Casting a Circle ~

Whatever technique or suggestion you use, once you feel empowered it's time to move on to the final step: casting a circle.

The idea is simple. The circle is like a stage, an area set aside for your magical work. Think of it as a place where it is safe for you to raise energy. Nothing that happens inside the circle can spill out of it, and in this space you are also safe and secure.

There are many elaborate ways to cast a circle and there are hundreds of books on witchcraft that will tell you the dos and don'ts. I believe that casting a circle is a personal thing and that the best way is to follow your intuition. If it feels right, then do it. You can't go wrong, because you're relying on a basic idea that has been used for many years.

If you like to mark things out, then you might like to use stones, crystals or candles to create a circle that you can actually step into.

If you prefer to imagine what the circle might look like in your head, that's fine too. You can do this by visualizing a circle of fire or light.

If you like words, you might prepare a speech or chant, where you invite the friendly spirits of the four directions (north, south, east and west) into the space to create a circle. All of these methods work and are equally powerful.

If you need a little direction, try the visualization below and see where it takes you. You can adapt this, and incorporate the physical aspect by marking out a circle shape if you wish.

1. Stand with your feet hip-width apart, shoulders relaxed. Close your eyes and breathe deeply.
2. Imagine a ball of light hovering above your head. This ball of energy is a gift from the universe. It is made up of positive and powerful energy that you can use to protect yourself.
3. Now picture the ball exploding so that it showers you with light that extends in every direction. See it pouring like a waterfall onto your head and then spraying outwards to create a circle of light that surrounds you.
4. Feel the warmth of that energy and know that you are completely protected.

5. At this point you might like to say something like "I am protected and blessed in this sacred space. I stand in the circle of light and grace."
6. Open your eyes and make a circular motion with your hands or turn around as if acknowledging the space set apart for your magical work.

Of course it's not always the appropriate time, space or situation to cast a circle. But there are still things that you can do.

1. Bring an image of a circle to your mind. For a few seconds see yourself standing in the centre. Know that you are protected and prepared. Now return to reality and get conjuring!
2. Keep a pendant, or a ring with a circular shape about your person. The simple gesture of touching this piece of jewellery will help connect you to the power of the circle.
3. Carry a stone that you have used when casting a circle before. Holding it for a few seconds will remind you of the experience and raise the right kind of positive energy.
4. Repeat in your mind "All life is a circle, and I stand in the centre, protected and strong."

Whichever of these preparation techniques you've used, you are now ready to begin!

CHAPTER 2

The Science of Magic

It might seem like a contradiction in terms to put science and magic together in the same sentence, never mind devoting a chapter to it. However, these two schools of thought in fact blend easily and complement each other. Science comes from the Latin word "scientia", which means knowledge. Its basic definition is that science is a system of acquiring knowledge through study and practice. Conclusions are drawn through experimentation, and knowledge is gained.

Magic too is a system based on acquiring knowledge through study and practice. Those who practice magic may spend years developing spells and rituals, and testing them to measure their effects on both themselves and their surroundings. Some might say that science is more evidence-based and that magic relies on a degree of faith and imagination. But then so does science. There are many scientists who would acknowledge that there is an element of creativity, of the great unknown, that seeps into their theories. So in a way the two schools of thought are similar, and it is this common ground that we can use to positive effect in modern magic, in our musings and everyday rituals.

New and exciting inventions spring up every day. The world is constantly changing and moving forward. So it makes sense that we should use this momentum and work with technological advances in a positive way.

Magic involves a degree of flexibility. Interestingly, the word "wicca" comes from the Anglo-Saxon word "wicce", which means to bend, and that's what we need to do in order to keep moving forward. We can combine the old ways with the new and come up with an innovative way of working magic that is in keeping with the world of today. Let's start by looking at some of our greatest inventions, and how we can combine them with a little everyday sorcery to maximize their potential.

Captivating Computers

Computers are at the heart of the new technological age. They've gone from being clunky thick-screened boxes, on chunky towers, to miniscule mobile laptops with vast memories and super-efficient speed. Whatever your choice of computer, there's a way to use it magically to get the things you want and enhance your life. Think for a moment about the power behind a computer, how at times it seems to have a mind of its own. In fact computers are a bit like brains: they are fed information, and they follow a thought pattern to produce a result or conclusion. Sometimes we overload them with information – we hit the "send" key too many times and click on the mouse as if we've got a nervous twitch, until the machine either freezes because it cannot take any more, or goes into meltdown.

Sound familiar? The human mind, too, is being constantly bombarded with images and details, but it can only take so much information. This means that we should really learn how to filter the messages that we send, and focus on the important ones, to help our mind avoid slowing down and eventually packing up completely. Computers offer up a wealth of possibilities. They're about speed, ease and efficiency. For example, they are obviously one way to access the internet. This modern phenomenon has

become a staple, an essential part of everyday life. Most people know how to navigate the World-Wide Web, how to communicate by email, and how to obtain information through search engines. The internet is a fantastic tool for communication, and the computer helps us use this to the best of our abilities. So it makes sense that the computer, and the internet, can help communicate our wishes to the universe, and transform our life.

~ A Few Things To Try ~

First a little preparation to make your computer – and your mind – run smoothly.

> Start by looking at what you have on your computer's desktop. Is it overloaded with items? Do you really need everything that's on there, or could it be filed away? The state

of your desktop is a good clue to the state of your mind. Streamline it, and you will not only feel better and more organized, but will also have a clean desktop to work from and create the things you want.

Next look at your email. How is your inbox? Cluttered, full of junk mail? Do you have files for different types of correspondence? If not, make some. Don't over-complicate this, though; all you really need is a file for work emails, a file for personal emails, and a file for magical emails. Yes, you did read that right.

Finally, make sure your computer's software is up to date and that it's vetted for viruses. Just as you would pay attention to how you feel – for example if you had a pain in your head, or if your thoughts made you feel a certain way – you should also keep your computer's mind and memory free from harm. Think of your computer as having a direct link to your mind and vice versa. You wouldn't want to plug your brain into something contaminated. Your computer is there to enhance your intelligence and make things easy for you.

TOP TIP

Crystals enhance the frequency and smooth running of computers, particularly quartz, so place one on or near your computer. Cactus plants are good for soaking up any negative energy, so it's a good idea to also keep one on your desk or nearby.

~ Mail Magic ~

We've all heard unfortunate tales of people who have vented their spleen by email, and then accidently hit the "send" button. At worst, their deepest darkest thoughts have gone global; at best, they've been received by the person they were aimed at. This can be highly embarrassing and painful for both parties. Imagine instead taking this scenario and turning it on its head for the best possible purpose. You can use email as a way to empower yourself, and help you tap into your inner goddess. All you have to do is write yourself an email and send it through the ether. It's that easy!

Imagine giving your inner goddess, the seat of your power and beauty, a voice. Imagine that she's a separate independent part of you, while still being the same thing as you – a bit like a superhero mantle that you can put on. Now imagine you are sending an email from your inner goddess to your real self. What would you say?

Well, for starters you might want to remind your real self of how beautiful, intelligent, talented and strong you are. So you could start by saying "Dear …, I am sending you this email to say – you are amazing. You are beautiful, talented …"

And so on.

This might seem like a strange thing to do, and also perhaps a little unnerving. This is quite natural; we're not used to being so positive about ourselves. We're quite happy to criticize, but when it comes bigging up our own achievements we struggle. Try to just accept those feelings and continue. When you have commended yourself for all the fabulous things that you are, think about the things you would like to be.

Say "I am strong, resourceful and flexible," or whatever it is that you would like to be, but make this statement in the present tense. This is not something you hanker after, this is something that you **are**. You just need to access the power within yourself.

Finally, end the email with a wish for good fortune and happiness. Something like, "I wish you a world of happiness and good fortune coming your way, as from today."

Now type in your own email address, and click "send".

Throughout history, letters have been traditionally used in magic to send good wishes and healing. Sending emails is obviously a new and super-quick way to keep in touch with others, almost like sending a letter but without the postage. Sending 'healing' emails is all about coupling a strong clear intention with the right words, and being able to picture exactly what you want. With this in mind, work on making your emails more effective by visualizing their effect. So if you're sending an email to secure some business, see in your mind's eye the receiver reading the email, being impressed and writing one back to say "Yes!". If you're emailing a friend and you want to cheer them up, picture them reading your message and smiling. It's as simple as that.

TOP TIP

To enhance the success of your message, burn cinnamon oil while writing, and send on a Wednesday when the gods of communication were traditionally believed to be at their sharpest.

The internet is a fabulous resource for images, and if you want to manifest something, it helps to have a clear image of it in your head. Use this screenshot spell to help work towards realizing your dreams.

Start by thinking of where you would like to be in a year's time. Think about location first of all. Where would you like to live? In what type of house? Who would your friends be and what would your personal situation be? Finally what job would you be doing, and what kind of lifestyle would you like to lead?

Come up with an answer to each of these questions, then go through the list and search the internet for images that help to inspire you and fit with your year plan.

When you have collected a range of images for each question, use them as screensavers, or alternatively print them off and create a huge wish map for your future.

These visual reminders will help you tap into your desires and think positive thoughts. Magic is about focus, intention and energy, so by using the power of your computer and the efficiency of the internet you can combine all of these things and amplify your wishes out to the universe.

TOP TIP

Whenever one of your chosen image flashes up (if you have them set as screensavers or wallpaper), put yourself in the picture and imagine you are living that life. Say confidently, "As I see, so mote it be." Then imagine breathing energy into the wish by taking a deep breath in and breathing out golden light that surrounds your computer screen.

Radical Radio

Can you imagine the delight of your ancestors when they switched on the radio for the first time? It must have been strange to hear all this sound coming from such a small box. It must have seemed like magic, and truly it is!

Radio waves are electromagnetic and travel at the speed of light. We can't see them, but they are there, and the evidence is in the music and chatter that we hear every time we listen to the radio. Proof again that science and magic are linked; just because we can't see something, doesn't mean that it doesn't exist.

Radios are an excellent tool for transmitting thoughts and energy. They are also good for honing psychic skills.

With the radio switched off, close your eyes and place your hands on it. Imagine you can hear what's going on inside the box. Let any words or music drift into your mind. When you get a clear snatch of either, turn the radio on and see if you've been able to psychically tap into those radio waves. You'll be amazed at how often the right tune comes into your mind, or a selection of words that you've picked up on are broadcast.

By the same token you can transmit thoughts and use radio waves to amplify them. With the radio on, turn down the sound and place your hands over the speakers. Form in your mind what you want to say; hear the words, but also try to picture them. Use images and symbols that match your intent; for example, if you want someone to call you, picture them, repeat the phrase "Call me," and picture a telephone and your number being dialled. The combination of all three things will help to send a powerful message to the universe. Spend a few minutes running over this in your head and imagine that your thoughts are travelling at the speed of light to the other person. When you are ready, turn up the radio and carry on your business. Let your request go, safe in the knowledge that it is travelling through the universe and will reach its desired destination.

TOP TIP

Develop your own theme tune. Everybody has one; it's the song that gets you up and out of bed. The tune that always gets you dancing and lifts your spirits. Make a personal pact that whenever it comes on the radio, whatever you are doing you will stop and enjoy the moment. Synchronicity plays an important part in magic, so embrace it, and if those lovely magical radio waves bring your song to you, make sure you repay them by dancing your socks off and enjoying the great mystery that is living!

Tantalizing Television

The television has long been a focal point for family life. It sits like a giant eye in the centre of the living room. It invades our life on a daily basis. In some cases it also makes appearances in the kitchen and the bedroom. This reflective square of light and pictures works its magic in a number of ways. It can be subtle, the background noise after a hard day at work, or it can take centre stage like a huge cinema screen, or the setting for a game on the Wii.

Let's face it, most of us have at some point in time enjoyed the idle luxury of putting our feet up to watch TV. There's nothing wrong with being a couch potato from time to time, especially when it can significantly boost your beauty regime! The next time you're slumped in front of the TV, try this out.

Relax your shoulders and lower your eyelids until the screen and everything on it becomes blurry. Now imagine that, instead of your usual TV programme, you are looking at a picture of yourself on the screen. If it helps, do this before you even put the TV on. At this point, if the light is right, you might already be able to see your reflected image.

The idea is that the image you see is a superhuman version of yourself; it shows you at your very best, looking totally gorgeous. So it's up to you. Make it as dazzling as you want. See yourself as you would like to be and imagine you are the star of the show. Notice how fabulous you look and how amazing you feel. Say, "As I see, so mote it be. I am free to be the best version of me."

Electrifying Energy

The discovery of electricity, and the invention of ways to harness it, has to be one of the best in history. The ability to power machines and lights at the flick of a switch is something we take for granted, but it's remarkable nonetheless. Imagine if you could "power" yourself in the same way – if you could give your energy levels a boost just by flicking a switch. With a little mind magic, this is possible.

The next time you turn on the lights, take a deep breath and imagine you have a light bulb attached to the top of your head. As you flick the switch on, a surge of energy travels through your body, lighting the bulb until it becomes a fluorescent orb. Feel the warmth of the light filter through your scalp, travel down your neck and around your body. Feel the buzz of this power working its way through your entire system. Enjoy these sensations for a few moments and breathe deeply.

You can do this exercise in reverse when you want to "power down" for the day and to help you sleep. As you switch the lights off, take a moment to visualize the light bulb on your head and imagine switching off the bright orb. Feel your body relax as your muscles grow heavy. Breathe deeply and clear your head. Do this for a few minutes before you go to bed to promote a healthy and peaceful sleep.

Cooking with Gas

Another great phenomenon that has become a convenience we all rely on: gas, and the ability to turn it on whenever we need to heat up our homes and cook our food. Gas provides essential warmth, and it is this comforting energy that can be tapped into to protect our homes and loved ones, and fire up the magic in our life. Interestingly, the word "gas" is often used in a different context, to mean someone who is "gassing" or talking a lot. It implies that they are babbling hot air, which may be true, but it also strongly suggests that what they are saying is backed by energy and enthusiasm.

Use the energy and enthusiasm generated by gas in your own home. On cold days, fire up the heating and as you do so, imagine a circle of blue light surrounding your home like a protective barrier. This light energy keeps those inside safe and away from harm. As you do this visualization, request the blessings of the spirits of the north, south, east and west. Ask them to guard and cleanse your home. At the same time, if you have some fresh rosemary, leave a sprig on every window ledge and hang some over your front porch or entrance hall.

~ The Magical Science of Appliance ~

Of course there are other, perhaps more mundane inventions that you can use in modern magic. Everyday objects can be put to use with dramatic effect. It's all about perception. How do you see these objects? Think first of all about what they do. What kind of service do they provide in your life? Then think about transforming this service, and making it useful in more magical ways. Once you apply the idea of magic – that there is an energy and a ritual in almost everything you do – you will see that smaller appliances have their uses too. All it takes is a little imagination, some willpower and a sprinkling of mind magic!

Looking for new ideas, solutions to problems, or perhaps you want to boost your creativity? Then look no further than your hairdryer on the table; it's the perfect magical tool to get your brain working.

HAIR-RAISING SPELL

Start by washing your hair, treating it as a magical ritual. As you massage the shampoo into your scalp, think of any problems that you need help with. If you simply want to stimulate your mind, rub your scalp and imagine that your head is gleaming with many tiny dots of light. When you've finished, tip your head upside down and set the dryer to work. Take a few moments, and as the hot air blows through your roots say, "I activate my mind today, each blast of heat will clear the way. Let answers come, and ideas stay. I'm wide awake in every way!" Is there something that you'd like to be rid of? Maybe you want to break a bad habit, or get over an obstacle. If so, then this is the spell for you. You'll need to buy, beg or borrow a shredder.

SHRED IT UP

Take a piece of paper and write down what it is that is bothering you. Put in as much detail as you can and include how it makes you feel. Push the paper through the shredder. As you do this, say, "I send you away, I am free from your hold. I break the pattern and the mould." Collect together the shredded bits of paper, and either bury them or drop them in the dustbin, repeating the chant above.

Who'd have thought that ironing could be a magical event? The ritual of taking an item of clothing, smoothing out the creases, and making it good as new, is one you can use to revamp your life.

IRON IT OUT

First invest in some rosewater. Its lovely scent is uplifting, and it can be spritzed on clothes and furniture to encourage love and harmony. Add a few drops of the rosewater to your iron. Take an item of washed clothing – something that you wear often – and begin to iron. As you smooth away the creases, say, "I smooth away the creases from my life, I bring the colour back into my world. I am restored from head to toe, renewed, re-vived, and ready to go!"

Mobile phones are probably one of our greatest inventions to date. So how about using your mobile to develop your psychic powers?

MOBILE MAGIC

Imagine you are sending a text to a friend. Get the blank screen up on your phone, but instead of typing in your message, pic-ture it on the screen. See the letters increase in size and bright-ness. If you can, imagine the message framed by gold light. Start with something simple like "Hello, how are you?" Focus on the message and imagine pressing the "send" button. Visualize the text disappearing as it would do if you had really sent it. Now forget the message and go about your business. Don't be surprised if your friend contacts you out of the blue. Keep practising and the universe will respond!

Blenders are great for making quick and healthy smoothies, but they can also be used to secure success and good fortune. Here's how!

BOUNTIFUL BLENDING

Mix together in the blender one chopped mango, a handful of strawberries, a squeeze of lemon, some ice and a sprig of freshly chopped mint. While blending, picture what it is that you want. So if you want a new job or promotion, see yourself in that role. If you want success in another area, then see it happening and enjoy those feelings of happiness. Say "Success is mine from this moment in time." Serve the drink in a sugar-rimmed glass and, as you enjoy it, continue to picture yourself with your heart's desire.

Are you suffering from a broken heart? Perhaps you want to break away from someone's influence on your life? Put them, and your feelings, on ice with this easy spell.

FREEZER FIX

Take a piece of paper and write down the problem or person that you want to get away from. Place the paper in a freezer bag and fill it with water. Add in a couple of drops of rosemary essential oil for protection. Put the bag in the freezer to chill. Say "On ice you remain, your power to wane. I release you from harm, I am free from your charm."

If you want to improve the atmosphere at home, here's one way to take the chill away and spread a little warmth. Stick on the radiators and get cosy with the ones you love.

RADIATOR LOVE

Before you put the heating on, fill a selection of dishes with warm water. Add a couple of drops of both lavender and orange essential oils to each dish. Place the dishes above or below your radiator in the living room, or in front of the fire if you use one. Put the heating or fire on, and let the scented oil cleanse the atmosphere of negative energy.

~ A Final Scientific Thought ~

It's easy to combine magic and science; all you need to do is look into the true nature of things. If something provides energy, then it can also be used to raise magical energy. If something provides heat, then it can be used to inspire action and movement. If something helps us communicate, then it can also help us communicate our wishes on the magical plane. The list goes on. Once you start to think in this way, you will realize that magic really is all around you, and that everything has a unique purpose that can bend at will. Science and magic are, after all, both creative art forms, both dabbling in the mysteries of life and the idea of cause and effect. Have fun exploring this world and coming up with your own rituals and mantras.

CHAPTER 3

Cook It Up!

Any magical practitioner knows that creating a spell is just like following a recipe. You gather the ingredients, follow the instructions, put a little love and effort into it, and hey presto, at the end you have the desired outcome. Whether it's a financial boost or an apple pie the idea is the same, but with magic the results can take a little longer. The kind of magic this book deals with is all about the mind. It's about using the human brain to its full potential, combining imagination, creativity and everyday items and rituals to manifest change. There is, though, still room for traditional ideas; in fact, as discussed earlier, mind magic is based on these traditional principles. With this in mind, I wanted to devote a chapter of the book to kitchen cupboard magic. This is not just magic made from recipes and ingredients that you can find in your store cupboards, although there is an element of that. This is about magic that you can do in the kitchen – little mind tricks that can help improve your day; rituals that you can perform with everyday items and ingredients; and ways to use the innate power of your house and home to conjure up a wonderful life!

The Ritual of Food

When you sit down to a meal, you are performing a ritual. You are doing something that you do every day, and it has a purpose; to give you energy. The more you make of this ritual, the more you get out of it. We are constantly being told to make time for our meals, to sit down at a table and focus on what we are eating, rather than mindlessly shovelling down mouthfuls while watching the TV. Eating with others is a way of bonding, and keeping the flow of communication alive in families. The food we eat is important, but the way we eat it and how we use meal-times is crucial too; these times can be put to good use, and can be turned into magical experiences. Here's how.

~ Breakfast ~

It's often said that breakfast is the most important meal of the day. This is because it fires up the metabolism, gives you energy after a long night fasting, and, if you choose nourishing morning foods, helps to beat mid-morning cravings. All of this is true, but breakfast also sets the tone of your day. If you think of your day as a story, the early, breakfast section is the part that sets the scene. It creates the atmosphere from which your story can flow. So, magically speaking, it's very important to get this right – to use this time to implant positive suggestions and raise personal power.

WHAT TO EAT

In magic, every food or ingredient has a specific energy vibration and is also associated with a different power. Knowing about these associations makes us able to link different food types to different areas of our life. For example if we want a successful romantic liaison, we can choose foods that will increase our chances of this happening.

Fruit

Fruit is good for you from a magical point of view as well as a physical-health one. The natural sugars it contains help draw positive energy into your life. Bananas provide energy and are closely linked to fertility and creativity. Strawberries, raspberries and apricots are associated with love and happiness. Lemon is a great cleansing juice, and orange, either in juice form or as a whole fruit, is wonderful for inspiring confidence and enthusiasm.

Nuts & Seeds

Nuts are great for communication. They stimulate conversation and can help you connect to others; that's why they're a popular and excellent party food. Peanuts, pecans and walnuts are good for success and self-expression, and almonds are associated with love.

Seeds are fantastic for an all-round energy boost and can also improve fertility. Choose sunflower and pumpkin seeds in particular to raise personal power and get the best out of your day.

Dairy

Essential for healthy bones, dairy comes in lots of interesting and magical packages. Cheese is very good for wish fulfilment; carve symbols representing what you want to achieve on a piece of cheese and eat while visualizing a positive outcome.

Milk is nurturing, and will give you confidence as well as soothing the mind in preparation for a busy day. Yoghurt combines well with fruit and nuts, making a highly palatable breakfast that will give a boost to your personal power.

Eggs are a "superfood"; not only are they healthy and filling, but they also can help release negative energy and cleanse your body and mind. Eat while imagining all the stress and worry being drawn out of your being.

WHAT TO DRINK

There are so many wonderful beverages with enchanting side-effects that you really can't go too wrong with your choice of drink. Steer clear of fizzy drinks though, as they drain magical energy. Coffee and tea are great early-morning pick-me-ups; and in magical terms the aroma of coffee brewing is a great stimulant, and promotes creative thinking. You don't even need to drink it to benefit! If you like the taste but don't want the caffeine, though, there are very good caffeine-free coffees in the shops. Hot water and lemon will cleanse the system; as you're drinking it, imagine the liquid travelling around your body flushing out toxins.

WHAT TO DO

It's not always practical to have breakfast with your family or household, especially if you're on a tight schedule. It is important, however, to make time to sit and eat breakfast. By making breakfast a significant morning ritual, you are making a statement that **you** are important, and that you are preparing yourself for the day ahead so that you can achieve all your goals.

Remember to chew each mouthful thoroughly and, as you do, start to run through your day. See it as a film in your head. See yourself going through every activity in the best possible way. When you have finished your breakfast, take a few moments to let your system start to digest the food. Close your eyes and make a positive magical statement, something like "Today is a brilliant day. I achieve all my goals and enjoy every second."

~ Lunch ~

This is the middle of your story, the part of the day when you will have experienced some sort of action. Things will be moving along, targets may or may not have been met. Your tale is unfolding. Lunch is a magical stopgap, a time for reflection on what you have achieved and what you still have to do. It's a time to gather your energies, and get those mind mantras working on your motivation.

WHAT TO EAT

Choose ingredients that aren't too heavy to stomach but that will sustain you through the rest of the day. Leafy fresh salads with some kind of lean protein are ideal; lettuce and spinach are linked to protection, and also have soothing properties to keep stress levels at a minimum. Tomato-rich foods are also good for inspiring strength, energy and motivation to help you get through the rest of the day. Any kind of lean meat, fish or eggs is a great base for a light lunch.

WHAT TO DRINK

Water is one of our greatest champions. Magically it's used in many cleansing rituals, and on a nutritional level it's excellent for keeping you hydrated and in top form. Drink it, splash it on your face, and run it over your wrists for a magical energy boost.

WHAT TO DO

Think of lunch as your stop gap. You might not have a lot of time, but make the most of it by taking a proper break. As you chew and digest your food, think positive thoughts and affirmations. You might repeat "Today is a wonderful day. Everything is going well. I am happy." If you can, spend a few moments clearing your mind of stress. An easy technique is to imagine you are sitting on a remote beach. The sun is shining and you can hear the sea lapping against the shore. Spend a few moments enjoying that peace and tranquillity, and then slowly bring yourself back to the present. This simple visualization will help calm your mind if you've had a stressful morning.

~ Dinner ~

The final meal of the day, and a chance for you to get together with the household, share your thoughts and feelings, and reflect on the day's events. Dinnertime is important, even if you spend it alone, as it enables you to evaluate what you have achieved. It's a chance to put the day to bed, whether it's been good or bad. Dinner is the frame around the picture of the day; you've taken the canvas, painted the picture, and now it's time to make it look its very best and hang it on the wall for all to see. It's a way of saying, "OK, so today I achieved this – now I'm going to leave it in today, give myself a pat on the back, relax and move on to tomorrow." In magical terms, dinner is a great time to give thanks and work spells for happiness, health and general well-being. You can also draw on the success of the day and reinforce any spells or mantras that you put in practice earlier.

WHAT TO EAT
Make a meal of it, and choose the things you love. Make dinner an event, even if you're the only diner. Remember that you've got through the day, and dinner marks your success. Set the table and visualize the kind of atmosphere you want to create. Make it special with personal touches. Play relaxing music and

encourage conversation. Hearty home-cooked meals are always good in magical terms, because you can put so much love and energy into them. Think about your desires as you create, and visualize them coming true.

WHAT TO DRINK

Some people enjoy a glass of wine with dinner as a way of winding down and making it an occasion. Wine is used in magic to give thanks and celebration, but water or juice are just as effective; go with your preference. Drink water with your meal to help you digest your food (and your dreams) and keep the flow of conversation going.

WHAT TO DO

It doesn't matter if you hate cooking; you can use pre-cooked meals in the same way. Just make the most of the microwave! Visualize yourself moving closer to your goals as the time ticks away, and when the final beep goes, see yourself hitting your dream. Make up cooking rhymes that work as mantras. Something simple like "I cook up my future, I create the best. With this meal I eat, I am truly blessed." Repeat as your food cooks, and then repeat in your head as you eat. Have fun with your food. It sustains you, and gives you the strength and energy to fulfil your dreams and create the future that you want.

Special Meals

If you want to celebrate something then a meal is obviously a fantastic idea, but you can also use special meals to help other aspects of your life flourish. For example, it's quite common for couples to share romantic meals in the early part of their relationship. This is seen as an essential ritual to encourage love and bonding. It's not so much about the food they eat, but the actual act of sitting down to a meal together, although there are specific foods that are associated with romance and thought to encourage the flow of love. Here are some ideas for magical meals.

~ Healing Dinner ~

You can create the perfect atmosphere for healing over dinner, whether your aim is to heal a rift or something more physical. Inviting friends and family who share a similar mindset will help.

TOP TIPS

Include nourishing foods, with lots of fresh vegetables and lean meat. With this more than any other type of meal, the emphasis is on the energy raised at the table, so start by making it look right. Include blue candles for healing, and yellow flowers to encourage positive vibes and communication.

Keep a jug of iced water on hand, and make sure that everyone has a glass. This is a good idea even if you are also drinking wine; water cleanses body and soul and will help with the flow of conversation.

Before your guests arrive, spend a few moments standing at the head of the table. Stretch your arms out and imagine that you can extend them to reach around the table as if you were holding it close. Visualize a ring of blue healing light circling the table.

Before you begin eating you might want to say a few words or a blessing. This doesn't have to be too complex or heavy.

∿ Business Brunch ∿

The idea of a business meal is to encourage communication, create good working relationships and secure success. With this in mind, choose food that everyone will enjoy eating and can dip into. Anything nut-based is good because nuts promote conversation, sun-dried tomatoes are great for success, and if you want to protect your assets and seal a deal, add a sprinkling of parsley to the plate.

TOP TIPS

Think about positioning. If you want to impress your boss, don't sit opposite; it promotes opposition and can be quite a challenging position. Instead sit diagonally from your boss, as this position encourages good communication.

Think about the colour scheme. Greens and golds work well together to promote success, so try to include these shades in your table decorations.

Visualize what you want to achieve. Before the meal, set aside some time to picture how you want it to go. See yourself getting your point across and impressing your guests. Picture a positive outcome and couple this with a magical statement like "Everything I touch turns to gold." Repeat this mind mantra in your head throughout the meal.

Eye contact is vital when you want to connect with people. Imagine there's a magical cord that stretches from your eyes to theirs. You can send very powerful thoughts along this cord, so as you make eye contact, think of your message. See it in the form of a picture or symbol and imagine sending it along the cord.

~ Romantic Supper ~

The power of the romantic supper is in the message behind it. It's about the time you spend together, and how you use it to bond. Choose foods that are easy to digest, and if you really want to spice things up, foods that you can feed to each other. Actions speak louder than words when you want to encourage romance.

TOP TIPS

Think about the way foods look. Taking the time and effort to present something really makes a difference. We eat with our eyes, and we are first attracted by what we see. Just as you would take time to make yourself look nice for your loved one, take time to make the food look delectable, and put love into your preparations. Keep puddings light. Sweet treats definitely encourage romance, but go for natural ingredients with lots of red and pink shades. Fruits like raspberries and strawberries are great for playful fun and attraction. Honey is also a good choice as it promotes love and beauty. While preparing the meal, think about the atmosphere you want to create. What kind of feelings do you want to encourage in your partner? Picture them enjoying the meal and having those feelings. Pour some love into it. Imagine a small tap in the centre of your chest. When you turn it on you get a stream of pink frothy liquid pouring from it. Visualize this covering your food. Visualize it covering everything to encourage a loving atmosphere!

Baking Spells

Baking is by far one of the most special things that we can do in the kitchen to enhance our world. Not only is it fabulous to eat home-made food and to share in the joy of its creation; there is also something very therapeutic about following a recipe. Perhaps this is because it's exactly the same as following a spell – there's a definite magical alchemy to the procedure: a wish, an energy, an intention and an outcome. This is why baking spells work wonderfully if you need an outcome fast. If there's an area of your life that has become stagnant, or you've hit what seems to be an insurmountable obstacle, then use a bit of baking power to overcome it. What's even more exciting is that you really don't need to do much more than put love and creative thought into what you are doing, and you will achieve great things. It's that easy!

~ Pies ~

If you want to create something in your life, then make a pie. These tasty offerings are built like dreams – the structure is simple, a filling and a topping that work together to create the perfect pie. The same can be said for the wishes that we have; it all starts with a desire, which builds in size because of the feelings we attach to it, and finally when we picture it, we see the wish coming true.

The secret to using pies magically is quite simply to visualize what you want as you make it. With each roll of your pastry, think of your dream and see it. As you add the filling, think of all the emotions associated with your dream and how

you will feel when it comes true. As you pop the pie in the oven, make your wish a statement of fact. So "I wish I had a wonderful new job" becomes "I have a fabulous new job." Then, just as if you'd made a wish while throwing a coin in a well and then left it there, leave the pie to work its magic. Don't stress about your wish, just let it go. Wait for the pie to cook, and when it's ready, eat, enjoy and know that your dream is on its way to you!

~ Cakes ~

There's nothing like a home-made sweet treat to melt the heart, and cakes are perfect for love magic. There's not a lot that you have to do; simply follow the recipe while focusing on your love request. It helps if you use flavourings that encourage romance, like vanilla, almond, or chocolate. Ginger cake will spice things up, as will a fruit cake. Victoria sponge with strawberry jam filling will also promote romance. The key is to visualize all the way through the process, then serve to your heart's desire. If you're thinking love on a much broader scale, then share the cake with some friends and family with a wish for happiness and love.

~ Scones ~

Scones have a bit of a reputation for being one of the hardest things to bake. Once you get the hang of them though, (and if you find a simple recipe), they are a real joy to bake. Scones are just like the challenges we face in life; at first they appear hard, and nothing seems to go to plan, but once we've mastered the basics, we can use the same method again and again to create a wonderful adventure of colour and taste. The true magic of scones comes in the extra ingredients that you add to the mix.

FLAVOURS

Cheese

If you're a savoury person, than this might be the scone for you. Cheese is great for wish-fulfilment and also to promote strength and protection because of its nurturing properties. The trick is to make your wish as you add and mix in the cheese. It really is that simple!

Sultanas/Raisins

A popular choice for scone lovers, a type of dried fruit is good for encouraging ideas. If you want to get creative and communicate your ideas, have a go at making dried-fruit scones. Imagine that each piece of fruit is a germ of an idea, and that you are stirring up your creativity as you mix the ingredients together.

Apricots

Great for romance and love, a few chopped apricots added to your mix will encourage positive feelings and also raise energy levels.

Coffee

Flavouring the mixture with coffee is not only an interesting slant on the original, but it also promotes hard work and motivation. If you've got an exam or a big meeting ahead, then these are the perfect scones to make and eat.

Tools of the Trade

When you're cooking or baking there are things you do as part of the process that can be turned into mind-magic rituals. Simple things that you may take for granted become effective tools to manifesting the things you want. Here are some of the best.

~ Mixing ~

Do you like stirring things up? When you think about what mixing actually means, you realize that it's about bringing all the ingredients together and whipping them into action. You have to add your own energy and intent as you stir, but it's worth it when you get just the right consistency. Because mixing can be quite active it's a great ritual to use when you need movement. If, for example there's not much happening in your love life, visualize a stream of adventurous dates as you mix. Imagine stirring up the powers of love, and visualize a swirl of bright pink emanating from your dish as you do this.

～ Chopping ～

Want to get rid of something from your life? Or perhaps there's a bad habit that you'd like to banish? Chopping is the perfect time to send that powerful message to the universe and set your magical intent in motion. As you chop, picture the thing that you want rid of. Imagine that you have it in your hands. So instead of chopping the carrot, you're chopping away at a cigarette. Each time the knife falls down, say "I release you from my life." Repeat this mantra over and over until you've finished chopping and there's nothing left.

～ Kneading ～

Got a problem? Then knead it away. As you smooth away the lumps with your fingers, imagine that you are smoothing away the obstacles in your life. Imagine you have the power of the gods, that this is your world that you are perfecting. You have all the ingredients to be a success; you just need to smooth them together and iron out any teething problems. Knead and visualize, taking each problem or stress and working it away to nothing. This is a really effective mind-magic trick to eradicate stress.

～ Simmering ～

When we simmer, it usually means our dish has reached the ideal temperature and we're quite happy to relax and let it bubble away. Simmering is a lesson in patience and belief; we know that if we wait long enough we'll have the perfect dish – we just have to stand back and have faith. In a way, magic is just the same. We make a wish, perform a bit of mind magic, and then we have to trust that it will all happen perfectly as we'd hoped. So any time you're simmering anything, remember all the magic you've sent to the universe and have the confidence in your dreams. Say something positive like "I trust the universe to deliver to me, all that is meant to be." Then relax, smile and wait for all those good things to come.

~ Boiling ~

Have you ever watched a pan of water boiling? The bubbles start to form, and then suddenly whoosh, they take over and there's an explosion of activity. If you need energy fast, use your boiling time as a simple ritual to increase your vitality. As the pan starts to boil, visualize the tiny bubbles of energy inside your body starting to pick up speed and power. Imagine these balls whizzing around your system until they burst out of the crown of your head in a shower of white light. Feel the excitement of all this energy spreading through you.

~ Grating ~

When we grate, it's usually because we want a sprinkle of something to add to a dish, whether that's during the making of it or as a decoration when it's finished. What you're doing is taking a block of something and reducing it to a more manageable size. Imagine you have the power of the universe at your fingertips, and use your grating time to spread a little healing love around the world. You can start small, with friends and relatives. Picture them standing beneath a giant magical grater, and then see them showered with love and positive energy. Once you've got used to this mind mantra, move on to bigger things. Take your street, or your town – or even the entire planet – and do the same thing.

~ Rolling ~

If you make a lot of pastry, this is something you'll be used to doing. There's nothing quite as therapeutic as rolling; taking a rough unformed lump of mixture and smoothing it out to a large flat canvas with your rolling pin. Make the most of this activity by seeing a picture before you. Imagine that your dough is a piece of art that reflects your life and how you would like it to be; imagine that it's a snapshot of the future. Spend a few moments visualizing every area. For example, if you've always wanted to live a peaceful life in the country, you might see yourself standing outside a beautiful cottage, surrounded by open fields, the sun shining and a happy expression on your face. When you have your picture, imagine sealing it around the edges with gold light and continue baking!

Kitchen Essentials

There are certain items and ingredients that almost every kitchen has. These are the everyday things that we use all the time, and that we can also put to magical use.

~Salt ~

In folklore, salt is a form of protection. Sprinkling salt on window ledges and at the bottom of doors was supposed to ward off evil spirits. In practical terms, salt enhances the flavour of your food, so using a little here and there will enhance power and energy. Combine with pepper, mix to form a grainy powder, and sprinkle it outside your home to promote feelings of safety and security.

~ Sugar ~

Sugar, whatever the type, can be used to draw things to you. A sprinkling here or there is like gold dust and will give any magical intentions an extra boost. You can also use sugar to "sweeten" things in your life, and you don't have to eat it to feel the effects. So if a relationship is struggling, then light a candle, surround it with a circle of the sweet stuff, and visualize things getting better.

~ Water ~

Pure and fresh, water is something we often take for granted – all we have to do is switch on a tap and out it flows. Water, though, is what sustains us. Without it we would not exist, so in magical terms it's one of the most important ingredients you can work with. Water magic helps us to tap into our emotions. Every time you rinse your hands, take a moment to feel the water doing its work. Imagine it being absorbed into the skin and cleansing you from the inside out. Collect fresh rainwater and freeze it into ice cubes to use in drinks and visualize the energy of nature working through your system to give you a boost.

~ Vinegar ~

The magical health benefits of vinegar make it a very powerful elixir. It can be used to heal cuts, sores, and skin conditions. It's good to use with food when you want to break down barriers, revamp your look, or promote beauty. A simple trick – when you next splodge vinegar on your fish and chips, make a wish for beauty. Imagine the vinegar cleaning you from the inside out, and helping your aura to shine!

~ Lemon juice ~

Great for cleansing you and your home, lemon juice (particularly if it's fresh) is a vital and very potent ingredient for energy, clarity and focus. When you add it to meals or drinks, it's like adding a magical elixir that will increase your personal power. As you squeeze the lemon, imagine that you are squeezing away the debris and stress from your life.

~ Honey ~

Not only is this store-cupboard staple great for health, it's also wonderful in beauty magic. Drizzle over food and eat while visualizing your beauty shining through. Alternatively, massage a little into skin, or use as a face mask. Leave for five minutes and then rinse off with lukewarm water. If you need a sudden burst of energy to motivate yourself, use honey to tap into the power of the bees that made it. Drizzle over cereals or yoghurt and give thanks to these wonderfully industrious creatures. Ask them to bless you with their energy, then eat and enjoy!

~ Rice ~

Rice is a cheap essential that can be used to bulk up a meal and provide sustenance. When you think about how it cooks, the fact that you only need a small amount because it absorbs the water and swells, then you will understand the magical properties of this ingredient. It helps in spells for abundance and wealth. If you need a financial boost, include rice in your diet. While it's cooking in the pot, see your bank balance swelling. A top tip is to take a jar and add a few grains of rice every day.

Make this a ritual, and every time you put more grains in say "I grow richer every day."

~ Scissors ~

We use scissors in the kitchen to prepare, to cut away excess packaging and open things up. Scissors are a wonderful magical tool; they can help to remove obstacles and "cut away" stress. The next time you have to use them, think about what you'd like to cut from your life. Say "I cut you free, I let you go." Then use the scissors as normal.

~ Cups ~

Cups are vessels for drinking and so they help us quench our thirst. They have also been used for centuries as a tool for scrying with tea leaves. The contents of the cup, though, are not as essential as the cup itself. For example, you could also tell the future with coffee granules, or even fresh orange juice with bits in. If you want to tap into your intuition and receive a little guidance, don't forget the humble cup. Use it with your regular brew. Drain the cup, turn it upside down, ask for a message and then have a look inside. The trick is to let any thoughts or impressions come without questioning them. Write down any shapes, symbols or pictures you see, and then have a go at making the connections between them.

~ Soup Bowls ~

You can never have too many bowls, and it's a good idea to have a range of sizes. You can use them to mix ingredients, and more importantly they make excellent scrying tools for predicting the future. Invest in a dark-coloured bowl and fill with warm water and a few drops of lavender essential oil. Inhale the aroma, relax and let your eyes glance into the bowl. Don't strain for images; just gaze, remembering to breathe, and let any patterns or symbols form. If you have a specific question, ask your intuition to guide you and look out for any signs. It helps to keep a note of anything that you see, even if it doesn't make sense at first; given time, you may start to notice a pattern or message emerging.

~ Cutlery ~

This might not seem obvious but there's plenty of magical potential in cutlery. Spoons are great for mixing things up, and forks are good for making a magical "point". Most powerfully of all, knives can be used to direct energy. Think of them as a modern-day wand. I'm not suggesting that you wander around waving a knife as this would be extremely dangerous. But in the right situation, you can use a knife or even a wooden spoon to direct energy into food. Simply picture the outcome that you want your meal to create. Take a deep breath, and as you breathe out imagine that energy and image pouring through the knife into your food.

CHAPTER 4

Home Improvements and Enchantments!

Magic is not limited to one place; it's everywhere. Wherever you go, wherever your imagination takes you, you will find enchantment. Everyday routines and items hold great potential if we can perceive them in new ways; the secret is to use your creative energy to make the most of the things around you. Your home is a powerhouse for magical energy. Every room is unique, and can be used in different ways to help you manifest the things you want.

Think for a minute about your favourite room. Why is it your favourite place to be? Is it because it conjures up a certain atmosphere? Perhaps it encourages feelings of peace and harmony, or you have lots of happy memories set in this room. Perhaps you see it as a safe haven and a place to retreat to, or maybe it's the space where you can truly be yourself. Whatever the reason, this room is the seat of your power. Use it this way. Treat it like an energy store. Spend time simply sitting in this space and replenishing yourself. Breathe deeply and enjoy your surroundings. Imagine absorbing the energy of this room. Feel the energy sinking beneath your skin and giving you a glow. Feel it sinking to your belly, just below your navel. Place your hands on this area and feel the warmth. Know that you are ready for anything, empowered and magical.

Now let's take a magical tour around the rest of your house and maximize your personal spell power!

Rooms and Their Magic

~ Living Room ~

Think about why we call this room a "living" room. It's because it's a place where we do most of our "living". Most of us spend a lot of time in this space, reading, talking, watching TV, relaxing, studying … We all come together as a household in this room, which creates and promotes a mixture of energies. It's a varied and very active atmosphere, and this atmosphere can be harnessed to fulfil dreams and get things moving. Rooms tend to hold on to things and absorb emotions, and because of this it's a very good idea to encourage a positive atmosphere in this main space that you do so much "living" in with your nearest and dearest.

TOP TIPS

Use flower power

Flowers are a product of nature and because of this they're linked to friendly spirits. Bring them into your house to add colour and raise positive energy. In particular, yellow flowers are good for attracting harmony; pink encourage romance and beauty; red are great for firing up passions; and white help to cleanse and promote feelings of tranquillity. Purple or violet flowers will help you tap into your higher self and improve intuition, while anything predominantly green will attract abundance and prosperity.

Bring the outside in

Stones, pebbles, pine cones, acorns and leaves are all a great addition to your living-room décor as they encourage the flow of energy and movement. Create potpourri-type nature displays in interesting bowls, or if you prefer, keep plants on your window ledge, and pictures of scenes from nature on the walls. Open the windows. Even if it's cold, a blast of fresh air from the outside will keep the room cleansed and help to get any stagnant energy moving. This is a great magical technique if there's an area of your life that seems to be in limbo: picture what it is that you would like to happen. Throw open your windows and your arms, and imagine embracing a blast of air and energy. Say "The wind of change brings hope and light, my life is moving, my future in sight."

Create an altar

This doesn't have to have any spiritual significance, and it doesn't have to look any particular way or like a "traditional" altar. An altar in this sense is simply an area of your living room that you dedicate to a specific aim. So if you want to promote love, you might create a small love altar using decorations and pictures that reflect your ideas of this emotion. If you create a money altar, you might decorate it with ornaments and pictures that represent wealth to you. An altar can be a corner of the room, a window ledge, even a coffee table. Have fun creating your altar and make it as personal as possible. Add to it often to keep the flow of energy moving, and whenever you do add something, remember to make a wish linked to your aim.

~ Bathroom ~

The bathroom is the place for cleansing. It's usually where we start the day and prepare ourselves, cleaning, preening and making sure we feel the best that we can. It's also where we go at the end of the day to wash all our cares away. So it makes sense to use this space as a spiritual retreat. The water element is key here; water to wash, water to refresh and water to flush away. In fact the toilet is one of the most useful magical tools you can imagine. If you want to release pain, fear or self-doubt, imagine throwing it in your toilet bowl before you flush. It's really that easy! Incidentally, in folklore urine was often used to mark territory, and it's believed that if you want to secure buying a house, then the best thing you can do (magically speaking) is to make a wish for success while using the loo in the house you want to buy!

TOP TIPS

Strengthen the energy of water and encourage it to improve cleansing power by decorating your bathroom in soothing sea shades. You can also bring elements of the ocean into the room by decorating with shells or stones found on the beach. Invest in essential oils, a great magical addition to any bathtime ritual. Choose oils that will help you create the right atmosphere and mood. If you're looking for something soothing lavender is a good choice; ylang-ylang is great for romance and juniper and bergamot are fantastic for increasing energy. Frankincense is superb for wish-fulfilment and geranium is perfect to help balance emotions. Add a couple of drops to your bathwater once it's run, breathe deeply and immerse yourself. As you do so, imagine the oil seeping into your skin and working its magic!

~ Bedroom ~

The boudoir is a complex place. So much goes on in this one room. It's a place of luxury and romance, a place to sleep and relax, and a place to dream and let the subconscious take control. Because of this, the room itself shouldn't be too busy or cluttered; there's enough going on in there without any extra stimulation. If at all possible, try to avoid having any electrical items in your bedroom as they can interfere with the ritual of sleep. When decorating, think about the effect you are trying to create and how you use the room. Combine colour and texture to create the perfect ambience.

TOP TIP

The bed is the focal point of the room. Depending on what you want to achieve, make this your central focus and treat it like a magical altar. Keep a piece of amethyst under your pillow if you want to encourage prophetic dreams. Mix dried cumin and chilli powder together in a small bowl and leave under your bed if you want to encourage hot action between the sheets! To promote a deep and relaxing sleep, add a couple of drops of lavender essential oil to a handkerchief and keep beneath your pillow.

Keep a dream jar on your bedside table and use it to make a wish every night. Take a penny and add it to the jar before you go to sleep. Make a wish at the same time. The idea is that your subconscious mind, which takes over while you

are sleeping, will send a powerful message to the universe. You can use the same principle to help with any problems or questions that you have; just ask your subconscious mind for help while you are sleeping, pop a penny in the wish jar, and leave the rest to your higher self! When the jar is full, put the pennies to good use – either buy yourself a nice pampering treat or buy some flowers for a friend or loved one.

~ Hallway ~

The entrance hall is the first thing you see when entering your home. It's all about first impressions, and the kind of initial feeling that you want to create for yourself and others. Use this area to improve the flow of things into your life; so for example if you want a more successful business, decorate your entrance hall with items that will encourage the flow of success and good fortune into your world.

TOP TIPS

Add water infused with fresh basil leaves to your floor wash. All you need to do is steep the leaves in boiling water for a few minutes, strain and decant into a bucket. Add in a squeeze of lemon and your usual floor cleaner. This mixture of ingredients will help to draw money and good luck into your life. Clean your entrance hall and front step with the mixture. Liberally drench your front path with the remaining water. As you do this visualize a stream of gold light travelling into your house and hallway.

Bells and chimes encourage harmony and good fortune, so if you can, hang bells and wind chimes in your hallway to draw in those happy vibes.

Use signs and symbols near your front entrance to attract the things you want. For example if you have always felt that the horseshoe was a lucky symbol, then invest in one, and hang it in your hallway or on your front door. Be creative and draw or paint symbols on floorboards or behind pictures. It doesn't matter that no one else can see them – the point is that you know they are there, and every time you pass the spot you will think about them and focus on those good feelings. Create an entrance ritual that you can use every time you enter your home. It doesn't have to be anything elaborate – something simple, like a short phrase that you repeat in your mind, coupled with a simple action, is perfect. The idea is to reinforce all the positive messages that you want to send to the universe. So perhaps you could make a point of skipping over the front step, and as you do so saying "I welcome the spirit of joy into my home." Or as you hang up your bag and coat, you might say "My home is my castle, my heart and my peace."

~ Garden ~

A garden helps you tap into the power of the earth. It grounds and restores you, while at the same time helping to instigate new ideas and keep the flow of creativity moving in your life. Not everyone is lucky enough to have an outside area, but if you don't there are still plenty of things you can do to connect with nature.

TOP TIPS

Keep an area of your garden wild; in other words, have an area where you just let nature take control and where the flowers and shrubs grow freely. This will encourage wildlife to prosper and the energy of the earth to flow in abundance.

Use this space when you need rejuvenation: stand barefoot on the grass and breathe deeply. Feel the power of the earth making the soles of your feet tingle. Feel it travelling up each leg, supporting and sustaining you. Imagine that you

are sprouting roots from your feet that reach deep into the earth and connect with the trees and plants. If you don't have a garden you can still do this exercise – do it in the back yard, or even on your doorstep!

You might not believe there are fairies at the bottom of your garden, but our ancestors believed that all living things had a spirit. Each plant, flower, stone and shrub had an energy associated with it. Tap into and encourage this power by making your garden more inviting. Include pretty stones and crystals in your landscaping; linked to the element of earth, they will keep the energy strong and grounded. Water features are also great because they keep emotional energy and love flowing, and represent the element of water. Wind chimes and bells are related to the element of air, and will encourage new ideas and creativity, and candles can be used to create a lovely warm atmosphere and for movement and protection, with their link to the element of fire. Again, if you don't have a garden you can still use some of these ideas; create magical window boxes with flowers, crystals and shells, or hang wind chimes and bells in windows and over your front door.

~ Throughout the House ~

Think about the things you do in each room, the everyday rituals that you take for granted, and be creative. Is there a way you can use them to transform your life? For example, cleaning of any kind can be used as a physical representation of cleansing in other senses. So if you want to clear away negative energy, just visualize this happening as you are scrubbing the floor, or dusting. Imagine that with each stroke or brush you are clearing the air of any stagnant energy. Be as specific as you like; for example, perhaps you're trying to shed a bit of weight. Imagine that as you clean you are also cleansing your aura and shedding those pounds. See yourself reduce in size and throw yourself into the cleaning process. The combination of movement and motivation works wonders!

TOP TIPS

Invest in special cleaning tools that you use for magical work – so have a separate feather duster, or a particular brush that you use to sweep away negative residue. If you're feeling really creative and practical have a go at making these tools for yourself, and before you use them make a statement to match your intention – something like "I use you to sweep away the stress of the day!"

Think about the impression you want to create with your home. If you were a visitor, how would you feel entering this house? If you want to create a light, happy atmosphere, for example, think of colours and textures that promote this feeling.

Give your home a name. Many magical practitioners use another name when they are performing spells. This name helps them to raise the right kind of power and energy; it's like adopting a persona that enhances their intent. You can follow the same principle with a house; give it a name that means something to you. You don't have to actually paint the name on the door if you don't want to – it can be a thing that only you and your loved ones know about. The idea is simply to attract the right kind of energy through the door.

～ Heartbeat of the Home ～

The key to using your home in a magical way is to think about what you want to achieve, and also what is missing from your world. If there's an area in your life that could be improved, look to your surroundings for clues. For instance, if you lack a sense of fun and spontaneity in your life, then it's probably also missing from your home. We often reflect on the outside what we are missing on the inside, so to attract something you need to start expressing it openly and sending a powerful message to the universe.

Follow this simple checklist to help you create mind magic rituals for your home.

1. Identify what is missing from your life, and then look for it in your home.
2. Think about what your heart's desire would look like if you were to represent it in colours, shapes, decorations or ornaments.
3. Introduce some of the ideas that represent your heart's desire into your home.
4. Create rituals using everyday objects to reinforce the things you want.

Remember, your house is a visual representation of who you are; make sure it paints the perfect picture and conjures up the atmosphere that suits you best.

CHAPTER 5

The Modern Goddess

The Goddess has always been an important part of magic. She represents the female aspect, the nurturing feminine energy that is all around us. The Goddess is in all of us, male or female, whatever our country or race. She is the divine spirit, the primordial earth mother, and we can tap into her power to help us manifest the things we want. Of course there's more to the Goddess than meets the eye. She is not an antiquated idea from the past. She exists now, in this vibrant, hectic modern world. She's as much a part of the busy city streets as she is of the undulating landscapes of the countryside. You can feel her energy anywhere, because most importantly she lives inside you. It's about finding your own relationship with her, finding a way of connecting to this wonderful feminine energy and making it real. So much magic is about perception – how we look at things, and being able to see the power and energy in the everyday. The Goddess is all around. You just need to choose how to see her.

You might prefer to think of her as an entity separate from yourself. You might see her as Celtic, Norse, Roman, Aztec or, if you're being really creative, part of some superhuman alien race.

You might see her as a part of yourself that you can tap into, almost like donning a superhero cape and becoming something else. It doesn't matter how you look at things; the most important thing is that you can connect to the Goddess's energy and use it to create positive change. You can look at the old rituals, and different mythologies, and bring them up to date so that they reflect the world you live in. There are no strict rules or laws. It's about making this work for you and your life, and making the best of yourself.

A good indicator of the best way to connect to this powerful feminine energy is to ask yourself, what do you think of when you hear the word "Goddess"? What image springs to mind? Take a few moments to do this now. Breathe deeply, close your eyes and think about the word, and let the images form.

If you have a very distinct picture of, for example, a Celtic woman with flowing hair and skirts, then that's fine. That's how she appears to you. If, instead you see a symbol, or a scene, that is also fine. Sometimes colours or animals might appear; again, do not judge. Let those pictures come and make a note of them.

The next stage is to explore the image and what it represents to you. Is it linked to a specific culture or mythology? If so, then do some digging and see what you can find out about the thoughts and beliefs of this culture. Who were their goddesses, and how did they relate to them? Did they see them as spiritual beings, or were they represented by real living people? What did they stand for, and what were they associated with?

You will find that as you look into different mythologies, each god or goddess had an area, or an idea, that they were linked with. Some were associated with animals or foods, for example. Gather as much information as you can, as this will help you tap into your personal goddess power. Trust your intuition, and even if the pictures that you see don't seem to relate to anything, make a note of them. They are still important because they will help you connect to the feminine energy within.

The following visualization is another easy way to invite the Goddess into your life. It's a great way to stretch your creative and intuitive skills, meet your inner goddess, and learn how to work with her on a daily basis!

~ The Crystal Palace ~

Start by finding somewhere comfortable where you won't be disturbed. To set the right atmosphere, burn candles or scented oils. Rose, lavender, geranium and orange are all excellent choices to help you relax and tap into your higher self. Find a space and sit with your shoulders back and relaxed. Close your eyes and breathe deeply, counting how long each breath is. Try to extend your outward breath by two counts. After a few minutes your mind will start to clear of clutter and you should feel calm and focused. When you are ready, turn your attention to the space behind your eyes. Imagine if you can a giant cinema screen. You can see a door projected onto this screen. Take your time and begin to notice things about this door. What is it made of? How big is it? Are there any patterns or pictures that you can see? When you are ready imagine that you are going to walk up to the door, open it and step through.

On the other side you see bright sunlight, a beautiful meadow and, in the distance, what looks like a giant crystal, the size of a castle. As you start to walk towards the crystal you notice that it is shaped like a palace, with turrets and arches. Every part of the crystal sparkles with dazzling beauty. Soon you are standing in front of it, and you can make out a huge door with the words THE SANCTUM OF THE GODDESS written in gold lettering above it. Take your time – take a deep breath and, when you're ready, go through the door.

From this point on, what you see is totally within your control. This is your inner landscape and your journey, so have fun and be creative. Perhaps the inside of the palace is like a comfy cottage, or maybe it's a lavish boudoir with lots of rugs and plush furnishings. Perhaps everything is made out of crystal and precious stone; the choice is yours. Take your time and explore this world. Eventually, at some point during the visualization you might meet your inner goddess. She might appear to you, or you might find her residing in one of the rooms. You might get a glimpse of her, or end up having an in-depth conversation; whatever feels right at the time. It really is up to you. Just enjoy the adventure, and try to remember everything that this dreamscape conjures up. This is your special place and a part of your personal imagination. You can come here whenever you want to connect to your goddess, or need to tap into her power. When you are ready, make your way out of the crystal palace, back through the meadow, and finally step back through the door in your head. Spend a few minutes focusing on your breathing, then open your eyes and relax.

It's a good idea to keep a journal of your visits to this place. It doesn't matter how you do this; you can write in detail, make simple notes or, if this works better for you, use pictures and symbols to describe what you have seen and learned. At first some of the things that your intuition throws up might seem quite bizarre, but this is perfectly normal. The subconscious mind uses a different language to communicate to the conscious mind. It uses symbols, patterns and pictures to connect with us, and it can take time to learn the hidden meanings behind this language. Making a note of what you see is the first step. Soon you will learn the connections and be able to understand what your goddess is trying to tell you.

If you can, try to repeat this visualization at the same time every week. Get into the habit of doing it regularly. The more practised you become, the easier it will be to tap into your goddess power at any time of day, simply by picturing her and the crystal palace.

The Goddess in Myth and Legend

As you start to look into Goddess myths and legends you will notice that although each one is unique, and has her own strengths and capabilities, she also shares common ground with her sisters from around the world. The Goddess encapsulates feminine energy. She is linked to love, freedom, and the ability to nurture the earth and those around us. Goddess energy is about making the best of yourself, and encouraging others to do the same. It's about being empowered, without being aggressive. Being strong without becoming overbearing. The Goddess aspect in our lives helps us to grow and become the very best that we can be.

Over the next few pages you will be introduced to a range of deities from different mythologies. Each one has a purpose and a list of associations. You may feel drawn to one or more of them. You may feel you have nothing in common with any of them. This is fine too! The idea is to absorb the information, see if any one piece stands out for you, and then work with it to tap into your goddess power. Look at some of the rituals and ideas, and try them on for size. Add your own slant to them. Experiment. The Goddess is alive, and she's developed over the years. She is as much about new modern traditions as she is about the old ways. So have fun and embrace the goddess within!

~ **Roman** ~

JUNO

This lovely Roman goddess looked after the hearth and home. Her name is linked to the month of June, when celebrations and festivities were carried out in her honour. Juno is a mother goddess; she is kind, caring and wise. She governs marriage and childbirth.

Associated with money, particularly silver coins, the hearth, fire and baking, Juno is also linked to prosperity and the idea that a combination of home, family and wealth make an abundant life.

Ritual

Find a pot and position it over your fireplace or near an oven. Every day, place a silver coin in the pot. As you do this visualize your home filled with love, a happy, healthy, abundant place where everyone feels secure. Say "I tap into the power of Juno, I ask her to bless this house. With every penny I offer up, may prosperity overflow in my cup." When the pot is full, use it to buy something for your home or family, then start collecting again.

TOP TIP

Baking is dear to Juno's heart, so have a go at rustling up some goodies to eat. Start with something simple, like biscuits or cakes. As you stir the mixture and roll it out, visualize what you want in life. Ask Juno to bless you with her power, and picture a positive outcome. Share your efforts and remember to visualize your wishes as you eat!

DIANA

This popular Roman figure was a nature goddess who roamed the forests and ruled the hunt.

Known for her strength and dexterity, Diana was also thought to protect wild animals. She had a twin brother, Apollo, the sun god, and was in some tales believed to be a goddess of the sun and moon.

Also associated with childbirth, fertility, strength and independence, Diana was often pictured with deer, bears or hunting dogs. She is associated with beech and oak trees, and sweet-smelling jasmine.

Ritual

Tap into Diana's power by getting out and about in the fresh air. Find some local countryside, a park or a garden and go for a walk. Collect fallen leaves, stones, acorns and feathers. Find a quiet spot, and use the things you have collected to mark out a circle. Stand in the centre, turn your face upwards and breathe deeply. As you take air into your lungs, imagine that they are filling up with the energy of your surroundings. Say, either in your mind or out loud, "I am a part of nature. I am connected to earth."

TOP TIP

Diana was known for her strength and flexibility. If you want to connect to her, try your hand at yoga or Pilates. Both of these exercise systems emphasize stretching and extending limbs and building up the strength of your inner core. Even if you don't want to do a class, just building some simple stretches into your everyday routine will help promote inner confidence and adaptability.

Try a simple stretch every morning when you wake. You don't even have to get out of bed. Just raise your arms until they are pointing upwards, stretch down with your feet and toes and hold this position for 5 seconds. Release and repeat again three times.

~ Greek ~

APHRODITE

Probably one of the most famous deities of love, Aphrodite is the Greek version of Venus. She is beautiful, alluring, and she radiates love. This enchanting goddess is associated with the luxuries of life. She is sensual and creative. On the negative side, she is known for her jealousy.

Aphrodite is associated with the hand-held mirror, which she uses to gaze at her beauty. She is also linked to apples – the fruit of love in Greek mythology – and red roses.

Ritual

A simple way to connect to Aphrodite's energy is to find an apple tree and sit beneath its branches. Even better if you're actually eating an apple at the time! With each mouthful, or breath, visualize yourself cloaked in soft pink light. When you have finished eating the apple, sprinkle the pips around the tree and ask Aphrodite to come into your world and fill it with her loving energy. If you're a city dweller, you can do this ritual indoors. Invest in apple-scented oil or candles, light, and follow the visualization above.

TOP TIP

Aphrodite doesn't fret about her curves. She embraces her feminine form, and enjoys the luxuries of life. Follow her lead by indulging in some of your favourite treats. Eat chocolate and strawberries, or apple pie. Wallow in a creamy bubble bath. Enjoy the delights of a massage. Most of all, celebrate who you are and recognize yourself as a beautiful being of light.

HECATE

This Greek triple goddess was often called the Queen of the Witches. Incredibly powerful, she was sometimes depicted with three faces, that of the Mother, the Maiden and the Crone. Hecate was known for her ability to see into the future, and her powers of protection.

Associated with owls, dogs and many other creatures of the night, Hecate is also linked to cypress trees, moonstone, the moon itself (particularly in its dark phase), keys and crossroads.

Ritual

The best way to connect to Hecate is to visit a crossroads at night. If you can't find a crossroads, instead choose a night when the moon is waning, or appears to have disappeared from the sky. Stand outside, and make an offering to the Goddess. This can be something sweet, like a cake, biscuit or a dollop of honey. If you have a problem or an obstacle that you want to overcome, Hecate can help. Ask for her blessing. Imagine taking the problem or issue in both hands and throwing it up into the air.

TOP TIP

Owls are the ultimate creature of the night. Like Hecate they can see the things we can't. Connect to her by wearing owl jewellery or collecting pictures of owls. Learn to stimulate your own psychic vision by picturing a third eye in the centre of your forehead. Imagine it opening, and absorbing messages and visions of the future.

~ Norse ~

FREYA

This warrior maiden had many talents. She was strong, feisty and also incredibly alluring; the tales tell of her captivating eyes. Apparently once a man had gazed into those eyes, he couldn't help but fall under her spell. One of the Valkyries, Freya spent her time collecting the souls of dead warriors and whisking them away to the feasting halls of Valhalla. She also charmed the dwarves into giving her their fabled necklace, Brisingamen.

Linked to the stone amber, and often pictured wearing the skin of a falcon, Freya is also associated with geese, cats, and the full moon.

Ritual

Tap into Freya's power by carrying a piece of amber. If possible, wear a piece around your neck. When you need to communicate with Freya, hold the stone gently against your throat and ask her to speak words of wisdom into your soul. On the night of a full moon, go outside and bury the amber in the ground. Look up to the stars and ask Freya to come into your life, to bless the stone with her powers and to give you the strength to achieve your dreams. The next day, dig the amber up, rinse in fresh water and wear with pride!

TOP TIP

Freya was often pictured wearing an ornate belt around her waist. She knew that the seat of her power was linked to her solar plexus. To give yourself an energy boost, invest in a belt, cinch it in tight to celebrate those curves, and place your hands over its centre. Imagine light pouring from your palms into your abdomen. Feel the gentle warmth fill your body. Say "Freya, I embrace your power and love."

~ Egyptian ~

BAST

This mysterious cat goddess was a powerful warrior and protector of Ra, the sun god. Bast celebrated all things feminine; she protected women and children, and cats. She was often shown as part-woman and part-cat, and just like her feline counterparts, she was lithe, independent, and incredibly alluring. Often called the Lady of the East or the All-Seeing Eye, Bast promoted joy and power.

Associated with cats, lions, perfume bottles, catnip, and the stones cat's eye and lapis lazuli, pleasure-seeking Bast is also linked to music and dance.

Ritual

Invest in a piece of lapis lazuli; this wonderful stone will help you strengthen your intuitive skills. Place the stone on your forehead and imagine a third eye in this spot. Then imagine the eye stretching open like a cat's eye. It's tuned into your sixth sense and will help you see into the future. Spend a few moments focusing on this area, and let any thoughts or impressions come to you. When you are ready, imagine the eye closing and remove the stone. Do this regularly to tap into Bast's powers.

TOP TIP

If you want to get along with Bast, then it's a good idea to get along with her favourite creature. Invite cats into your life. Encourage them into your garden by growing or sprinkling catnip. Keep cat images and symbols about your person, and start to think like a moggy – be curious, follow your instincts, and be proud of who you are. Most importantly, always take time out to stroke our feline friends.

ISIS

Known as the Mother of Life, Isis was a goddess of magic. She ruled over her people in a gentle way, acting as teacher and friend. She was associated with life, death and rebirth. Her magical knowledge made her an impressive sorceress, able to breathe life into the dead. Isis was also considered to be extremely beautiful and the mother of all goddesses.

Associated with the symbol of the ankh, cows, the full moon, corn, wheat and rivers, Isis can be useful if you want to improve your magical knowledge and wisdom.

Ritual

Breathe new life into your world with this simple ritual. In the morning, throw back the curtains, stretch your arms out to the sides and breathe deeply. Imagine a ray of light bursting from the centre of your chest. See it shoot out to the world, spreading joy and happiness. Now imagine it coming back to you, hitting your chest and filling you with warmth and energy. Ask Isis to fill you with her power and knowledge as you embark on the day.

TOP TIP

Isis was a great teacher; she enjoyed imparting knowledge and wisdom. If you want to tap into her power, get into learning. Pick a subject you know nothing about and research it. Even better, take up a course or sign up for a workshop. Foster the spirit of learning and encourage others to extend their knowledge too.

~ Celtic ~

BRIGID

This beautiful Celtic fire goddess ruled over the forge, and was also linked to poetry and childbirth. Brigid was renowned for her powers of inspiration, and poets and bards would seek her help with their creative efforts. A sun goddess, her gifts are light, energy and creativity. Some tales tell that wherever she walked flowers would spring up at her feet.

She is associated with fire, candles, sunrise, wells or springs, bees, lambs and dandelions. She is also linked to the sound of bells ringing and whistling.

Ritual

Invite Brigid into your life. Throw the doors and windows open at first light, and walk through your house ringing a bell. If you can't find a bell, a whistle will do. Pass through every room and make a sound; as you do this ask Brigid to bless your life, to give you inspiration and energy to move forwards.

You might also want to have a go at creating a Brigid cross that you can hang over the entrance to your house. This is usually made using reeds, and you can make it as simple or as complicated as you would like, depending on how handy you are at arts and crafts.

TOP TIP

Be like Brigid and encourage the flowers to grow. You don't have to be a whizz at gardening. Invest in pots and plant some wild flowers. Choose lots of blue and purple colours to encourage bees and butterflies. Sprinkle wild flower seeds outside and put up a bee box if you have the room. Take inspiration from the outdoors and just as the flower grow, so will your ideas and passion.

MORRIGAN

This enchanting triple goddess is often linked to death and rebirth. Said to hover over battlefields in the form of a raven, Morrigan would collect the souls of the dead and guide them on their journey. She rules over rivers and seas and is also linked to prophecy, magic, and the psychic arts. Morrigan governs the fates, and it was believed she would hand-pick which individuals were to die by washing their clothes in the river.

Morrigan is also associated with the crow and raven, rivers, streams, the moon, and horses.

Ritual

This is a great ritual that will help you to feel powerful and protected throughout the day. Stand with your feet hip-width apart. Turn your attention to your shoulders and imagine two balls of energy, one on each of your shoulder blades, buzzing away. Now visualize these balls turning into glossy black wings that extend from your shoulders, and feel them stretch around your body to cover you like a cloak. Ask Morrigan to protect and steer you in the right direction as you go about your business.

TOP TIP

Washing clothes might not seem the most magical thing to do, but it is a way of using an everyday ritual to tap into the mighty power of Morrigan. Choose some garments to hand-wash, and as you plunge the clothes into the water, imagine all the negative energy and thoughts being washed away. Say "I am cleansed, I am renewed. Born again with power of Morrigan to fulfil my destiny!"

～ West African ～

OSHUN

This Yoruban goddess of love and beauty celebrates all the good things in life. She is associated with happiness and abundance. Linked to fresh running water, Oshun can be found near streams and rivers. She is a sensual goddess who enjoys the freedom of movement, including dance and music. She also has powers to heal the sick and watch over the poor.

Associated with water, honey, cowrie shells, oranges and the colours yellow and gold, Oshun is sometimes pictured with the tail of a mermaid.

Ritual

Write a message to Oshun, petitioning her for guidance. Take the paper and place it in or under a shell. Next light a yellow candle and place it before the shell. Close your eyes and imagine you are standing at the edge of a stream. Gaze into the water and let any images or patterns arise. Spend a few moments in this meditative state. When you are ready open your eyes, let the candle burn down, and keep the shell and note in a safe place.

TOP TIP

Become a honey goddess like Oshun by using this wonderful natural gift to help you connect to her beautiful spirit. Eat it every day and add to hot water for the perfect early-morning pick-me-up drink. To promote beauty inside and out, add a spoonful to the running water of your bath and immerse yourself. Enjoy this sensual skin treat.

~ Hawaiian ~

PELE

The fiery goddess of the volcano, Pele is hot hot hot! Thought to reside wherever there's volcanic action, Pele can appear either as a young beautiful woman dressed in flowing white robes, or as an old crone, asking directions and a light for a smoke. Some tales say that those who helped the old woman would be blessed, and those who ignored her would come to feel the force of her anger. Pele is all about passion, movement, energy and action.

She is linked to fire, ash and dancing and often appears with a small white dog at her side.

Ritual

Tap into Pele's energy by lighting a candle. Spend a few moments watching the flame grow and rise. Imagine that the flame sits inside you, in the area just above your navel, the solar plexus. Feel the warmth as it burns. Feel it grow and twist, filling you with energy and power. Now imagine it extending out of the top of your head, stretching up to connect to the universe. Ask Pele to help you be true to your life's passion, to follow your heart, and put plans into action.

TOP TIP

Pele connects to the rhythm of the earth. She dances with passion, and enjoys the freedom that movement can bring. Stick on your favourite song and dance. Doesn't matter where you are! Make a point of doing this once a day – let the beat take over, let yourself go, and really sink into the rhythm. Make this your power song, and play it whenever you need a pick-me-up. Say "I am free to dance to the beat of life!"

Goddess Gifts

Whichever goddess you feel drawn to, the common denominator is that they all celebrate their femininity. They embrace their personal power, and they're not afraid to use it to enhance life and improve the lives of others. Generosity of spirit is the key to tapping into your goddess power. What is it that you're good at? What do you enjoy doing? We all have talents and strengths that we can use to make life more magical and to manifest the things we want. Goddess power is about using our abilities in a positive way. Think of your own unique talent as a gift from the divine. It doesn't matter what it is, it's still a superpower, because it makes you who you are. As long as you enjoy doing it, and it has a positive effect, then it's a gift.

For example, you might be an excellent gardener. You might love the outdoors and have green fingers. If this is your gift, tap into your unique power and grow your own plants and herbs for magical spells. Make your garden an enchanting retreat after a hard day's work. Help others turn their outside space into something magical; spread the love by sharing your ideas and your wares.

If writing is your thing, get creative. Start a journal or a collection of poetry. Share your thoughts with others and write poems as gifts. Encourage others to have a go, and start a writing circle. Use words in creative ways to manifest the future you want, by telling stories in your head and then on paper. Start a story box, and fill it with tales for the future, things that you want to happen and wishes for others.

Have fun with this. Ask yourself, if you were a goddess what would you rule over? Would you be a moon or a sun goddess? Would you rule over the seas or the earth? What animals would you be linked to and why? This will also give you a clue as to your unique strength. Allow yourself the luxury to daydream. This might seem foolish, but it's essential because it helps you to relax, to manifest a positive future, and to perceive things in new ways.

Finally, change your attitude. Tapping into goddess power is about believing in yourself. You are special, you have your own gifts. In the modern world of ten thousand things it's very easy to forget this and to get bogged down in the mundane, because of course we have to get on with life and do the everyday things that matter. But there's no reason why we can't sprinkle a bit of magic along the way. Whatever you are doing, remind yourself that you are special, that you have the Goddess within you. Do things with purpose, even if it's something as simple as getting in the car and going to work. Do things with thought; think about the effect your actions have on others. Are there ways that you can improve what you are doing to help your surroundings? Why not carshare? Give someone a lift and minimize the effect on the environment. When you grab your morning cuppa, do a coffee run and treat your colleagues. Always make sure to smile. Make eye contact. Make a magical impression, and send people positive thoughts. Little things matter. Little things can enhance your world. Remember, you are a goddess. You have the power to change things for both yourself and others.

However you choose to work with a deity and embrace your goddess spirit, the key is to do it with love. There are no hard and fast rules; it's about your personal relationship with the feminine, nurturing energy inside. So have fun exploring this fascinating area, and make your own rules as you go along!

CHAPTER 6

The Tales We Tell

Words are magical. They have a power that, if used in the right way and combined with stories and memories, can help us manifest the things we want. Magic doesn't have to be complicated, and in our modern and complicated world, it's good to know that we can introduce a little enchantment into our lives just by using our imagination and enjoying language. Putting the right words together in stories works like a charm, because the stories we tell ourselves are the most powerful. They affect the way we think, feel, and the way others interact with us. Life is a constant narrative, and sometimes it can feel as though we are going along with a story rather than being the master storyteller, but you can take control back and create great things.

The first step is getting to know how tales can help you. Get used to how stories work, and learn what makes them special. Once you've discovered the hidden symbols and clues within the texts, it's easy to tap into their power.

Once upon a time, far away in a world of fairytales there lived a beautiful princess … sound familiar? It's the stuff of childhood memories, those enchanting bedtime stories that we loved and listened to with fascination. But there's more to these tales than meets the eye. Look a little deeper, forage further in the depths of the dark forest and you'll be surprised at the magical secrets you unearth.

Fairytales have an almost dreamlike quality because they're steeped in symbolism. They are very visual, and their imagery is

one aspect of them that helps us identify and understand their magical symbols. Fairytales across cultures and history also contain archetypal narrative events, themes and characters that can be understood at a deep level and applied to all aspects of our lives.

The idea of transformation features in most fairytales. It is the idea that we have to go through something, to transform ourselves, in order to become the person we are meant to be. In 'Sleeping Beauty', for example, the poor girl suffers at the hands of a terrible curse when she reaches a certain age. She is instantly plunged into sleep for many years. This is her period of transformation. She must learn, grow and develop until she is ready for the prince to find her and bring her back to life. Many people believe that this is a reference to puberty and the changes we go through to reach womanhood.

The character of the wicked witch or queen appears again and again in fairytales, and is a representation or suggestion of something dark and sinister.

These dark elements within a tale represent the shadow side of our personality. They might be traits that we try to keep under wraps, or the aspects of ourselves that hold us back. Think in terms of bad habits, or behaviour patterns that can be destructive. According to the stories, the best way to overcome this dark side is to acknowledge that it is there, rather than pretending that it doesn't exist. Think 'Little Red Riding Hood'; anyone can see that the wolf is dressed up as Grandma, but the main character pretends it's not true, because up until that point she hasn't wanted to face it.

Stories like this show us that we must be brave and not follow the path of self-delusion; instead, we have to face things – go into the forest at night, or stand up to the evil monster. In the end this path, no matter how tricky to navigate, will lead to salvation.

Just as fairytales contain dark elements that represent negative character traits, they also offer good things, like the kind, caring fairy godmother. She reaches out and offers hope when we least expect it. This symbolizes the spirit of human nature; it shows us that even when we are in the darkest places, we can still find something positive to focus on. She is our feminine wisdom, our instinct and intuition, and she often comes with warnings. In 'Cinderella', for example, the main character must be home when the clock strikes midnight. She must not stay too late, or overdo her spell in the spotlight. The message here is that we should trust our intuition. We know what is right and wrong, and to ignore this inner wisdom is foolish and dangerous.

So these fairytales or wonder tales, as they were called by the Victorians, hold the key to some interesting truths about life and the psyche. They may appear on the surface to be simple stories of good versus evil, but the moral dilemmas faced in them contain some very large truths and can be used as examples for learning and personal transformation.

The following visualization is a great introduction to working with stories. Use it to explore your inner landscape, and unlock magical secrets of personal transformation.

> Start by closing your eyes. Take deep breaths in and out until you feel every part of your body relaxing. When you are ready, imagine that you are standing at the edge of a magical forest. It's night and the moon illuminates your path. You enter the forest and take the path to the centre. The stars are twinkling overhead and you feel safe and relaxed. Remember that this is your story and you are in control at all times.
>
> You see lights darting among the trees, and realize that they are fairies and tree spirits dancing. In the heart of the forest there is a clearing, with a small wooden house sitting in it. The door of the house opens and there on the front step stands an old woman. She walks towards you and smiles; in her hands she has a small box. "This is the gift I give to you, from the depths of your soul," she says. Open the box and look inside. What do you see? Perhaps it's a jewel or a crystal, maybe it's a flower, or it could be a handwritten message or a word. Let your imagination take over as you examine the gift and what it means to you.

Spend as much time as you like in the forest. Explore and have fun. You may meet other magical beings; you may even go on an adventure. This is your story, so enjoy! When you are ready, retreat by returning down the same path as before; stand at the edge of the forest and feel the light of the moon bathing you from head to toe in its powerful cleansing energies. Now open your eyes and make a note of everything you can remember.

Twists, Turns and Crises

One of the keys to understanding fairytales is to look at the narrative thread. Consider how the story is put together; the twists and turns are clues and represent different stages in our lives and developments within our psyche. To get the most from a story we must consider its ebb and flow. Everything happens for a reason and we can learn from the pattern of events. Start by asking what happens to the heroine? Does she begin in a position of power and then lose it along the way? Perhaps she starts off in a bad situation and through a series of challenges improves her circumstances?

In every good tale there is always a point of crisis; this could be an insurmountable obstacle or an outside influence like an evil queen. It could be that the heroine makes a mistake, and allows herself to be taken in by these influences, or that she is a victim of circumstance. Either way, it is what she does from this point on that really counts. By looking at the general trends of the story and how the character deals with them, the overall lesson becomes clear. The next step is to think about how you can apply this lesson to your life.

Consider the following questions:

1. **Can I see myself in the main character?**
2. **What type of strengths and weaknesses do we share?**
3. **What kind of obstacles do I face, and how are they similar?**
4. **Can I learn anything from the character's actions?**
5. **What is the overall message of this story and how can I apply it to my life?**
6. **If I could sum up this story in one word, what would it be?**

Heartbeat of the Tale

The heartbeat of a tale is the core truth hidden within the plot, and every storyteller knows the power of finding it. Without it the story lacks passion and meaning and becomes a skeleton of sentences. The heartbeat can be summed up in a word and will be different for everyone, depending on how they see and respond to the tale. Stories and words are uniquely personal, and a set of words can conjure up very different pictures in different people depending on, amongst other things, their life experience and personality.

> Draw three boxes of the same size. Each one represents a section of the tale: the beginning, the middle, and the end. In each box write three sentences that sum up what happens in this part of the tale. Keep your sentences short and simple. Think about how the story moves along from the beginning to the middle and then to the end. Draw two lines linking each box. This is the bridge from each stage of the story. Now think about a few words or a short phrase that might

help to move the story along, and write it in the space. Next think about the point of crisis: what is it? Remember, this is the point from which the tale can go in any direction. Finally, think of one word that sums up the story for you. It can be a statement, or an emotion. For example, you might think Cinderella is about beauty – the beauty of the spirit and how it shines through in the end. Perhaps you think it's about trust – trusting in yourself to overcome obstacles and achieve your dreams. Once you discover what the tale means you can establish whether it can be used as a tool for self-development and transformation. Consider whether this is an area that you need to work on. Stories have a way of calling to the soul, and you will instinctively know if a tale is right for you.

~ Stories and Their Meanings ~

Here are some well-known fairytales and some suggested meanings. The best interpretations are personal, so keep an open mind, get reading and have fun!

RED RIDING HOOD
Accepting and facing inner fears, negative traits

SLEEPING BEAUTY
Transformation, developing as a woman, change and maturity

CINDERELLA
Embracing power and learning to rescue yourself

RAPUNZEL
Being imprisoned by beliefs, expectations, finding freedom

SNOW WHITE

Innocence, jealousy, self-reflection; how do we see ourselves and how do others see us?

BEAUTY AND THE BEAST

Self-sacrifice, and looking beyond appearance to the true heart of something or someone

THE LITTLE MERMAID

Loss of identity and creativity, giving up personal power

THE RED SHOES

Loss of control by stifling your true nature

Symbols and Archetypes

Fairy stories are like onions; they have many layers to peel away and explore. Packed to the brim with potent imagery, these tales are a treasure trove of symbols and archetypes that appear again and again. These symbols can be used in magic; to understand and work with them you just need to identify the most obvious ones and the messages behind them. Here are some common ones.

THE BEAUTIFUL PRINCESS

Innocent and lovely, the princess is often related to the child archetype. In most fairytales she goes through a period of transformation as she matures. She represents our journey into womanhood and symbolizes spirituality and the need to nurture the creative side of life.

THE EVIL STEPMOTHER

Cut from the same cloth as the wicked witch, the stepmother figure is seen as vengeful and full of hate. She represents oppression, and censorship, not only from outside influences, but also from the limitations we put upon ourselves.

THE FOREST/WILD WOOD

The wild nature of the soul, the shadow self that lives in all of us. This relates to the side that we keep hidden. Exploring the wild wood can lead to some surprising discoveries about what makes us tick. The wood represents unknown territory and facing our fears.

THE FAIRY GODMOTHER

The mother figure, nurturing and protective. The fairy godmother relates to the magic inside, the part that embraces our best bits and celebrates them. She is the inner goddess, the quiet voice of wisdom that begs our attention.

THE HANDSOME PRINCE

The hero/heroine. The prince represents courage and the ability to stand up for ourselves and achieve our dreams. Often used as a catalyst for change, the prince's kiss breaks the curse. He is the inner strength and clear vision that helps us to overcome obstacles and move on.

Ask yourself the following questions:

1. Do you identify with any of these archetypes?
2. Which one would you most like to be like, and why?
3. How can you be more like this archetype?

There are some things you can do to link to the power of the archetype that represents your ideal. Start by reading as much as you can about them. Think about how they act, and see if you can adapt your own behaviour to be more like them.

Spend some time visualizing yourself in a similar role. Take a story that you know well and put yourself in it. Take on the role of the archetype who saves the day. Imagine how you would think and feel and enjoy those sensations. This is incredibly empowering, particularly if you need a confidence boost before an important event or meeting.

Picturing yourself in character. Imagine looking in a mirror and seeing this new revamped version of yourself smiling back. Take note of how you look and stand. Imagine stepping through the mirror and absorbing the essence of this new you, so that you feel more confident, and have all of the characteristics of the archetype.

Common Pitfalls in the Land of Make-Believe

Along with archetypes and symbols, wonder tales tend to include a number of common pitfalls that we can also identify with. These stumbling blocks can reveal the way forward and deliver powerful messages.

~ The Long Sleep ~

Falling asleep for hundreds of years seems to be a hazard for those fairytale babes! It's the curse that befalls both Sleeping Beauty and Snow White, to different degrees. The long sleep, as it's often called, suggests a period of withdrawal from the world. This can be through choice – withdrawing into oneself – or can symbolize being forced into a passive position. It suggests having no control over events in your life. It can also mean a period of no change, where everything remains in limbo. Sometimes it is easier to stick with the status quo, but as Beauty learns on awakening, even a difficult change can bring wonderful things!

If you feel as though you are going through a "big sleep" phase, turn it around. Re-imagine the story. See yourself woken up, not necessarily by a handsome prince (unless you want to!) but emerging like a butterfly from the chrysalis to be the best that you can be. Repeat this visualization every day, and soon you will notice a change in your attitude and movement in your life.

~ Pricking Fingers ~

This is a powerful metaphor. The obvious meaning is of personal harm, doing something that causes you pain. Sleeping Beauty pricks her finger and it makes her withdraw from the world and fall prey to the evil fairy's curse. The message here is not to give up your power, whether that's to a situation or a person.

Imagine that power is a gift and see it as a small gold box. If you feel you have given your power away, picture yourself taking it back. See the box in your hands. Open it and feel the energy and power surge through you.

~ Eating Poisoned Apples ~

There's an element of temptation that comes with the poisoned-apple syndrome. Sometimes we are attracted to things and people that we know aren't good for us. There's a risk attached to our actions, but desire overrides common sense. Fairytales warn us of taking a step too far and losing sight of our true nature.

The easiest way to use this scenario to your benefit is to imagine a fruit tree heavy with different types of fruit. You may be attracted to the poisoned apple, whatever that is in your life, but there's plenty of choice out there, and a selection of fruits that **won't** kill you. So if you feel tempted to do something that you know you shouldn't, picture yourself throwing the apple away. Return to the fruit tree and choose something else that you know you will enjoy!

~ The Red Shoes ~

The fairytale of 'The Red Shoes' captures perfectly the sense of losing all control. It shows how through loss, or starvation of the soul, a woman can be tempted to grasp for substitutes, things that will make her feel better, but that can also do harm. Bad relationships, alcohol and obsessive behaviour all fall into this category. Just as the child has her handmade red shoes taken from her, as women it's easy to lose our way and not be true to ourselves.

Use 'The Red Shoes' as a cautionary tale about things that are no good for you. Light a black candle and, using red ink, write or draw on a piece of paper the name of the thing that you feel has a hold on you, or provides an unnecessary crutch. Burn the paper in the candle and scatter the ashes.

Then, to turn things positive again, imagine you too own a pair of red shoes. (If you actually do own a pair, put them on!) These are magic shoes and unlike the pair in the tale, with their destructive influence, they will ensure that you are on the right path. Stick on your favourite tune and dance. Enjoy those feelings of freedom and say "I follow the path that is true to me, I dance, I sing, I enjoy being free."

Shape-shifting Stories

You can work with existing tales and use their potent imagery and symbols to transform your life, but how about creating new stories to bring about magical change? It isn't as complicated as you might think. You can use fairytales to change the shape of your life. The key is how you relate to them.

~ Empower and Imagine ~

Think about a fairytale that you identify with. For example, if it's 'Cinderella', take a few moments to think the story through. Imagine you are in a cinema watching it on the screen. See yourself as the main character. When you reach the point of crisis, freeze-frame and pause the film. This is the point in the story where a resolution is needed; something has happened, some kind of dilemma for the main character, and the rest of the story is about how they solve this problem. From this point on, the story could go anywhere. Rather than playing the rest of the film to its familiar ending, you're going to come up with a new one.

In the case of Cinderella, what would happen, for example, if she never met the prince? How would she resolve the problem of the ugly sisters and rise above her situation? See yourself, as Cinders, gaining strength and confidence. Stepping out of the drudgery and becoming dynamic and accomplished. Hold this image in your mind, and replay the film several times until you automatically think of the character and the story in this way.

Now relate this to yourself whenever you start thinking about the future, and how finding your perfect partner will make you complete. Take a step back. Repeat this affirmation: "I love being myself. I am happy and confident in my own skin. I am complete." At the same time bring to mind the image of the empowered "Cinders" character above to remind yourself of how wonderful you are.

~ Character Traits ~

Think about the character that you most identify with, and make a list of their positive character traits. So if you choose Snow White you might say she is kind, warm, unassuming, hard hard-working, light-hearted etc. Remember that you probably identify with this character because you hold some of these traits yourself. So celebrate those good points and congratulate yourself on being fabulous!

Now make a list of all the traits you might consider negative. So perhaps you think that Snow White is gullible, weak, or naive. Look at each point on this list in turn. Do you consider yourself to have this quality? If the answer is yes, then think about how you might change that. What would make you feel less gullible or naive? What steps could you take to feel strong? Perhaps you might want to do some physical exercise to improve your strength, or take a course on asserting yourself. You might not have to do anything drastic; simply acknowledging that you think this is a problem will help you to recognize and break the pattern.

~ Turn it Around ~

Another simple way of repositioning yourself using fairytales is to take back the power and look at the story from a different perspective. So for example, we tend to assume that Cinderella needs the prince to escape her life of drudgery and become a princess, but what if it's the other way round? Think about it for a moment. The prince needs a bride. He's looking for love too, and he's searching for the right type of person. He throws a ball to find this perfect love, and then spends the rest of the story parading around with a glass slipper trying to find the woman who has captured his heart. So who needs who more? Perhaps the prince feels that he needs his soulmate to complete him; if this is the case then these two are very well matched.

You might not want to be exactly like a princess from a fairytale; however, there are some characteristics that you can adopt to help you feel positive, powerful and enchanting. Learn here how to express your fabulous feminine side.

TOP TIPS

Repeat several times "I am perfect. I am complete. I love myself." If possible, find a mirror and say it like you mean it, with a dazzling smile to finish!

Every day when you wake up, take a moment to think ahead. See all the things you wish to accomplish today, and visualize yourself being a wonderful success at all of them.

Step outside your comfort zone. Do something different, no matter how small – take a different route to work, or say hello to a stranger you see every day but have never spoken to. These small changes will boost your confidence and help you enjoy the wonder of life.

Daydream, but imagine it as a glossy star-studded film, with you as the A-list star of the moment!

Wear turquoise – either the stone or the colour – for strength and to help you express yourself in a clear, confident and positive manner.

Write your own fairy story. Take a pen and paper and make up a story where you are the central character. Have fun with this and give yourself magical powers. Perhaps you have suitors queuing up for your hand, but in the end you decide you're better off without them. So you live happily ever after, ruler of the kingdom and in charge of your destiny!

Make up a princess power oil. Take half a cup of sunflower oil, heat gently in a pan and add in a couple of drops each of rose, lavender, and ylang ylang essential oils. Other good oils for your princess power mix include patchouli, geranium, bergamot and orange, but this oil mix is all about you, and should also include your particular favourite oil if you have one. Do a bit of research into which of these oils goes well with your favourite. Let the mixture cool, and either massage it into your wrists or add to bathwater for super-smooth skin and instant sex appeal.

Spellbinding Story Circles

Set up a creative storytelling circle and make it a social event. The idea is that you get to work your mind magic in a larger group, exercise your creative muscles and have fun. All you need is a group of willing friends and a little imagination.

Take it in turns to start a story and include yourself as the main character. You can set it in any genre and make it as fantastical as you like, but the aim is for the story to be empowering. So make it clear from the start that, although the tale can go in any direction, and quite often does when other people get involved, it has to have a positive and inspiring outcome. In other words, the main character is always the hero or heroine of the tale. Take turns, each person in the circle adding to the tale until you all feel that it has come to a natural conclusion. If it helps, ask the group to write words of inspiration on pieces of paper and then put them in a hat that each person can dip into when it's their turn to speak.

Another great idea to create story magic is to work with a group of close friends. Get everyone together at a specific time and explain that you're going to have some fun telling stories. Use it as an opportunity to release the past and overcome fears and phobias. So if there's a particular event in your life that you have been thinking of as negative, turn it around. Tell the story but make it about a different character, thus taking yourself out of the picture, and give it a positive ending. Retelling the story in the presence of others is powerful, and using this technique helps you to distance yourself from the event and see it in a different light.

If you really want to perform some powerful mind magic, agree with your story group on a particular wish or aim. For example, you might be desperate for a new job, so explain to the group beforehand that you are all going to be telling a combined story where you, as the central character, find and secure the perfect job. Go round the circle with each person telling part of the tale, as before, until you reach a successful conclusion. If you focus your creative efforts and work together you will raise enough energy to send a powerful message to the universe!

CHAPTER 7

Picture This!

If there was ever a superpower alive and well and living in the world today, it would be the power of visualization – the ability to picture things with the mind, look into the future and visualize exactly what you want to happen, and then power that image with enough energy to make it real. Witches often chant "As I see so mote it be." In other words, they've performed the spell, they've mixed the ingredients and now they are seeing the outcome they would like. As they have seen, so it shall be. This belief, this inner certainty, ensures success. This is what visualization is all about.

It's a skill to think visually, and one that many people find it hard to acquire or develop, but there are things you can do to improve your picturing power. However, let's not get too caught up in the details here. Fantastic as it is to be able to picture things to such an extent that they become real and virtually 3D, it isn't essential to making your magic work. You don't have to be picture perfect; the most important thing to remember is how you seal the deal. At the end of visualizing what you want, you have to believe that it has already happened. You have to bring it into the present, imagine you have it now, and believe with every fibre of your being that it is yours. If you don't, then it's almost like saying "OK, this is what I want, but I don't quite believe I'm good enough to get it." By saying this you are putting it out of your reach.

So how can you hone your visual skills? Here are a few tried and tested techniques.

Apple of My Eye

Find an apple, or any other piece of fruit. Place it on a work surface in front of you. Take a few minutes to study it: pay attention to its shape, size, colour, texture, markings, scent … Take in as much detail as you can about this apple. Next close your eyes, take a few minutes to clear your thoughts, and then bring the image of the apple to your mind. See it in as much detail as you can. Now imagine taking a bite out of the apple. Feel it in your mouth. Imagine chewing it. What does it taste like? Enjoy all those feelings.

Finally, open your eyes and reward yourself with a real bite of the apple!

Don't worry if you find it hard to picture the apple or hold the image for long. Visualization takes time and practice. The key thing is to have some sort of picture in your mind, even if it's inexact or only there briefly, and to be able to experience the feelings of connecting with that apple.

Sitting Pretty

Take an everyday object, for example a chair. It could be a chair that you know well – your favourite one – or a chair that you have seen somewhere and liked. It could be the kind of chair that you would like if you could create the perfect perch. It's entirely up to you.

Close your eyes and picture it in your mind. Start by thinking about what it looks like; its size, shape, colour and so on.

Then move on to visualizing more detail. What is it made of? Does it have any unusual markings or decorations? What does it smell of? What does it feel like? Create that picture in your mind and hold it there for as long as possible. Imagine how you would feel sitting in that chair right now and enjoy those sensations.

This exercise combines the skill of visualization with stretching the imagination muscle, as this time, unlike in the exercise above, you don't have the object in front of you. This doesn't matter, though, because visualization is not a rigid practice; it's a flexible fluid skill and you can go anywhere with it. Think of visualization as being like a mathematical equation. It combines the skill of picturing with use of the imagination, a huge dollop of intention and energy, a sprinkling of emotion to make the experience real, and finally an injection of self-belief. So: Picturing + Imagination + Intention + Energy + Emotion + Self-Belief = Manifestation.

Here are some tips to help you get started on the road to creating a fabulous future.

Start small

Every morning, visualize something that you would like to happen that day. Don't make this a big deal; pick something little, for example the man who serves your coffee gives you a big smile, or you get the parking space that is always taken.

Don't strain

If the image is not clear, don't force it. Visualization is about being relaxed and confident, and the more you strain to see something, the less likely you are to be able to conjure up the image.

Don't give up

If you can't see any results it doesn't mean it's not working. You just need to keep practising, increase the energy and intention behind the thought, and trust in your innate power.

Engage your emotions

Many people forget to include how they feel in the visualization, but it is really important. This emotional engagement is what makes the experience real and sends a powerful message to the universe.

Daydream a little

This really helps with your visualizing skills. Take the pressure off by letting go of the idea that you have to create something that's "real" and just have fun imagining your wildest dreams. At the end of the day, the only difference between daydreaming and visualization is direction.

Tell stories

Get into the habit of seeing life like a collection of tales. Tell yourself stories of how you want things to go. Create an inner dialogue with yourself, and imagine you are telling the tale of your life. You are the central character and you can go anywhere and do anything.

Believe in yourself

Being able to picture what you want is a fantastic skill, but as with most things in life, you need to have other things in place as well to make it work, and self-belief is top of the list. Some visualizations take time to manifest, so instead of getting anxious or impatient, look for signs that things are happening. They will be all around you.

Visualization Vitality

There are many things you can do to develop and improve your visual skills. Anything that enhances your visual skills and encourages you to retain images better works well.

～ Magical Mind Mapping ～

Mind mapping is an excellent tool that you can use for any area of life. Start with a large sheet of plain paper. Think about your heart's desire – what are you trying to achieve? If you can, sum this up in one word. So you might pick "wealth" for more money, or "love" if you're looking for a soulmate. In the centre of the paper write this word, then draw some lines leading out from it. Think about pictures and images that represent what you want. So you might have pictures of cars, money, nice clothes, or a new house to represent wealth, or pictures of hearts, flowers, cherubs, champagne and couples together to represent love. You don't have to draw these images if you don't want to; find pictures in magazines and newspapers, or on the internet. Cut and stick the images onto the mind map like a collage. Don't worry too much about how it looks; the important thing is stimulating your visual senses.

When you've done this, move on to the next level – draw more lines leading from the pictures and begin to think about how you might achieve these scenarios. What will bring you more wealth? If it's a new job or a pay rise, find pictures or words that represent this. If you'd like to win the money, then you might put up an image of the lottery, bingo, or a competition. Don't limit yourself to one way of achieving your dream; think of as many as possible and find pictures to represent each one. Soon you will start to connect the pictures and come up with many different ways of making your dream a reality. When you have finished, pin up the mind map somewhere that you can see it. Every time you come across an image that fits in with your plans, stick it up there. The more you add, the more movement and action you invite into your life.

~ Storyboard Sorcery ~

Another powerful tool for visualizations to help you define your ideas and plans is a magical storyboard. Start by thinking seriously about what you want in life. Ask yourself that question. Now imagine you are writing a story about someone who's just like you and who wants the same things.

Draw a series of squares on a sheet of paper. Each square is going to include a picture or a symbol, drawn or selected by you, that sums up this stage of the journey; for example, if you want a new job, the first picture might show you scanning the newspaper for jobs. In the second picture you might be circling a position. The third might show you posting your application, and the fourth might show a happy smiling face as you get a call inviting you for an interview. The fifth could show you in the interview, looking confident and relaxed, and the sixth might be a picture of a glass of bubbly to celebrate your new job. Under each picture write either a short snappy phrase that sums the picture up, or a few key words. Remember to include emotions; for example if you want to inspire confidence say "I am full of confidence." Finally, think of one word that sums up the entire storyboard – the word that captures the spirit of the new-job board might be, for example, "Success". Write this word in big letters above your storyboard.

Place the storyboard in a prominent place, somewhere that you will see it every day and be reminded of your wish. Pinned to a fridge or on a noticeboard are good places for your storyboard. Every time you look at it, run through each picture, repeating the words and the key phrases in your mind. Finish by saying "As I see so it shall be."

~ Memory Box ~

Memories make us who we are. We all have good and bad experiences in our memory, and too often we focus on the bad ones. Learning to focus instead on all the good things that have happened in your life will give you a stronger sense of self-belief, raise your energy levels and make your visualizations more effective.

Create your own magical memory box. Find a box you like and fill it with mementoes of days out, achievements and experiences that you've enjoyed. Photographs, pictures, poems, quotes, letters – all of these things can be added to the box. You can also add interesting finds like stones or crystals, or special ornaments, ticket stubs from events that you've attended, and anything that reminds you of how special you are and how wonderful life can be.

Make a point of regularly adding to the box and going through some of the tokens already inside.

Another idea is to dip into the box once a week, pull something out, and say or write a few words about it. Bring the experience to your mind as if you were watching a film. Run through it, and when you reach a point in the trail of events that sums up what this memory means to you, freeze the picture. Hold the image there and surround it with gold light. Say "I experience all the good feelings from this memory, I love my life and it loves me."

This kind of activity is a great pick-me-up at any time, and if performed on a regular basis will improve your self-belief and confidence.

Six Essential Visualizations

Once you have honed your visual skills you need to try doing some visualizations. Start simple; remember, visualizing doesn't have to be complicated. You're not rewriting *War and Peace*! Below are five key visualizations for you to try. Have fun with them, practise and experiment. If some of the settings don't feel right to you, change them. You write the script, after all, so give yourself free rein.

~ Love Bucket ~

This visualization helps to attract love and a new relationship. Rather than focusing on a specific person, though, it is about visualizing yourself as loved and lovable. This leaves the universe open to surprise you with the perfect soul match.

Imagine there's a bucket balanced above your head, full of thick pink goo that looks a bit like pink custard. Now picture the bucket tipping over your head. Imagine the goo covering you from head to toe in pink. Hold this image in your mind. Say "I am loved and I am lovable. I radiate love at all times."

~ Cosmic Cash Machine ~

Wouldn't it be great if we had our very own cosmic cashpoint, where we could draw out any amount of money at any time? This visualization will help you attract more money into your life.

Imagine standing in front of a cash machine. Insert your card as you would normally do, and when it asks how much money you want, type in the amount. Be bold and ask for what you want (without being too greedy!). Picture typing in the figures and see them come up on the screen. See the machine produce the money and watch yourself taking it. Feel happy and secure in the knowledge that you have everything you need from the universe.

~ Spotlight Success ~

Whether you fancy your fifteen minutes of fame, or you'd just like a glimmer of success, this mini visualization can help.

Imagine you are standing on a stage. The spotlight falls on you, the lights go up and the audience begin to cheer. They are applauding you for your success. Take a bow – enjoy the adulation! As you look up, see yourself projected on big screens around the room. Notice how wonderful and radiant you look. The crowd goes wild with applause. Take a moment to say thank you to your fans, and to thank the universe for whatever it is that you want to achieve, but remember, in this visualization you have already achieved it! Feel like a million dollars, and know that you can do anything you set your mind to.

~ Energy Dial ~

This nifty visualization is quick and easy but has a powerful effect on the way you feel.

Visualize a small dial like a thermostat, just above your belly-button. Imagine turning it clockwise, and as you do so begin to see your aura glowing. You can see it surrounding you, a soft white light. Continue to turn the dial and notice that your aura is getting brighter, until the light is dazzling. Notice how this makes you feel, how full of energy and vitality you are. When you get to a point where you feel supercharged with energy, place both hands over the area and imagine setting the dial at this level. Now go about your business with renewed vigour!

~ Pennies from Heaven ~

This effective visualization is similar to the cosmic cash machine above, as it encourages the flow of money into your life. You can, though, also use it to invite in success and recognition.

Imagine you are standing in a wood. You see a shaft of sunlight spilling through the trees. You walk towards the spot where the light is beaming down, and stand beneath the warm glow.

Suddenly there's movement in the air. You look up to see notes dropping from the sky, hundreds and thousands of pound notes, gold coins, jewels and stars. The sunlight grows in brightness, bathing you in glory as these wonderful gifts from heaven fall at your feet.

⁓ Healing Hugs ⁓

There's nothing nicer than a hug, and the power of touch is incredibly healing. Use this in a visualization to help those who you care about. Bring the person to mind and picture them standing before you. Imagine you are walking towards them. Throw your arms open wide, smile and give them a big hug. As you do this, picture a ball of blue light surrounding you both. Feel the warmth of the hug and make a silent wish for health and well-being.

The Sorcery of Synchronicity

Visualization works on many levels and once you start to practise this magical art form, you'll notice changes happening in different areas and different ways. Some things happen almost instantly and some take time; it all depends on the nature of your request and situation. The important thing is always to be open and ready for the universe to fulfil your wish. Again, it comes back to the idea of expectation, and knowing in your heart that what you have pictured will sooner or later come to be.

Synchronicity plays a large part in this type of magic, so it's important that you are aware of subtle changes, of the signs and symbols that destiny throws in our path. Once you recognize those signs, it's important that you act on them.

~ Intuition and Action ~

To embrace the synchronicity of life you need to activate your intuitive skills. In other words, follow your instincts. Tune in to those gut feelings, and go with them. Learn to distinguish between good and bad sensations. Your intuition is an internal alarm – it can alert you to something wonderful, and it can make you aware of potential harm.

Start by paying attention to your solar plexus. This is the area just below your breastbone and above your navel. Every day, spend a few minutes focusing on this area. Imagine a ball of energy buzzing in this space. See it as a small white flower bud. Imagine the petals opening slowly until the flower is fully open and you can see a light shining in the centre. Doing this will activate your intuition.

Take notice of any sensations in this area. Do you get a warm fuzzy feeling when you're talking to a particular person? This could mean that they are a good influence and will be important in your life. Perhaps you get the same feeling about a situation or an opportunity. Again, this is a positive sign. Do you get a tingling of excitement when you're offered the chance to do something new? This could mean that it will be an adventure and that you should definitely do it as part of your journey to success. At the other extreme, perhaps you meet someone new and feel a sharp stabbing feeling or slight queasiness in this area. This could mean that you should be wary of this person. Start to learn what each sensation means for you and use it as a guide as you encounter new people and situations.

~ Signs and Symbols ~

Once you become confident about using your intuitive skills, you'll start to notice recurring signs and symbols in your life. Again, this is a personal thing and what works or makes perfect sense for one person might not be the same for someone else. For example, one woman might have an affinity with crows; whenever she sees a picture of a crow, she knows that she should investigate further. So she always looks at books with crows on the cover; if a crow turns up outside her window, she takes it as a sign that good news is on its way; and if she hears a crow cawing, she takes that as a warning. Another woman might feel drawn to the number 11 because it's been significant in her life. Her child was born on the eleventh day of the eleventh month, or her new house is number 11.

You will already have things in your life that are important to you; signs, symbols, words, numbers, colours. It's all about paying attention and learning more about what these things mean to you.

~ Making Connections ~

When you embrace synchronicity, you naturally start to make connections between things. You look for signs to steer you in the right direction. You are open to coincidence and see the magic in it. Say for example you are looking for a career change. You dream about a mountain and see yourself standing at the top. The next day you miss your usual bus home from work and have to get a different one. As you're sitting on the new bus, you notice a poster with a mountain on it. There's a slogan that says, "You can reach the top with us!" You read further and discover that this is a poster for an open evening at a local college. Coincidentally, this bus takes a slightly different route home – straight past the college in the poster. You have two choices: you can either ignore the synchronicity and head for home, wondering why nothing special ever happens to you, or you can seize the chance – get off at the college, go to the open evening, and sign up for a course that you're drawn to, which could ultimately result in a big career change.

This is how synchronicity works. It's about paying attention, recognizing the signs from fate, and taking a risk. It has a snowball effect; the more you do this, the more exciting things happen, the more energy you build up, and the more effectively your visualizations work for you.

Open yourself to the flow of synchronicity with this simple visualization.

> Stand beneath the shower with your eyes closed. As the water hits the top of your head, imagine that it's a spray of white light sent from the sky. Feel it travel through your scalp, down past the back of your eyes, into your neck and throat. Feel it flow all the way down your spine, along each limb, until eventually it emerges from the soles of your feet. At the same time picture the white light cascading around you to form a cloak of light that protects and replenishes your spirit. If it feels right, say a few words, perhaps "I am open and ready for the magic of synchronicity in my life. I go with the flow and follow my instincts."
>
> Do this first thing in the morning to set you up for the day, or before you go to bed to encourage prophetic dreams.

TOP TIPS

Be open
You may decide you want something, and perform the most wonderful mind magic, coupled with a beautiful visualiza-

tion, only to find that it doesn't really work as you'd expected. This is because you're not really open to it. For example, you may say you want love, but you're secretly scared. So instead of drawing a love that's free and available into your life, you attract someone who is already attached. Always make sure you are open and ready for your heart's desire.

Be brave

As your picturing skills develop, you will notice that things happen for you. You will see the signs. It's up to you to follow them. This can be daunting, as it stirs up change in your life. It means going with the flow, and not necessarily knowing how things will turn out. Take a deep breath and be bold!

Be creative

Don't limit yourself. Throw the door wide open and go for the bigger picture. The world is a big place with lots of opportunity. So rather than saying, "I want to be a successful horror writer,". Say, "I want to be successful in all my creative endeavours" and see what happens. You may become a successful horror writer, and you may also find other interests in the arts.

Be magical

Believe in magic and it exists. Life is magic. Living is a magical experience. Every day brings new and exciting opportunities. Try to look at things differently; see the magic in the city streets, rather than the humdrum. See the magic in the smile of a stranger. Appreciate life and it will appreciate you.

Be unique

You are an individual and you know what works for you. Just because one person believes that a feather is a message from the heavens doesn't mean you have to think the same way. If something unusual happens, if a sign or symbol keeps repeating in your life, ask yourself what it means to you personally. What do you associate with it? This will give you a clue as to what the universe is trying to tell you and if synchronicity is at work.

Final Word

In mind magic, how you finish is as important as how you be-gin. We can start with the best intentions. We can research, vi-sualize, raise energy, and believe in a positive outcome, but what happens when the magic works? We celebrate. We acknowledge our blessings, and most importantly, we share our good fortune. Once you have the tools to make your life a better place, you can use them to help others. This is essential, because what we put into the world we get back, and there is nothing more magical than the feeling that you have helped someone else.

The joy we get from receiving is made even more special by giving. If you really want an enchanted life, then be sure to put energy into others. Spread the love and the magic around and it will come back multiplied. This is an old rule, but it works. This is because any kind of magic is a transaction; it's a negotiation, using energy. So it makes sense that the more you put into some-thing, the more you will eventually get back.

Every time you use mind magic, you're increasing your power. Every time you help others you're adding interest to all that positive energy you're generating. Think of it as a cosmic bank account. You add to it, and slowly but surely the amount increases. The interest goes on as a small thank-you for banking with the universe, and voilá, you get a wonderful surprise at the end of it all!

So, go forward. Have fun using the techniques in this book. Experiment and enjoy the vibrant force that is your imagination, and the innate power of your spirit. Make your world a better place, and make wonderful mind magic!

Astrology Reading Cards
by Alison Chester-Lambert

*This card deck was designed by a top astrologer (founder of the
Midlands School of Astrology) as a simple, easy-to-use pack
that utilizes the archetypal energies of astrology to answer
questions about the Present and the Future. Select a card from
each of 3 separate sets – the Zodiac Signs, the Planets and the
Houses – and then use the guidelines in the book to interpret
the answer – just like going to a professional astrologer!
Set consists of 36 cards with colour illustrations and a
96 page paperback with 37 colour illustrations.*

978-1-84409-581-0

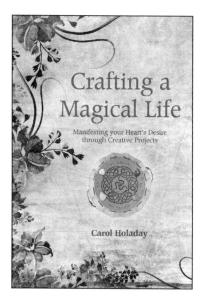

Crafting a Magical Life
by *Carol Holaday*

Crafting a Magical Life *outlines twenty magical / spiritual
items that you can craft yourself, thereby utilizing the focus of
your desire and intention to improve your spiritual connection
and bring the mystical and magical into your life. Each chapter
contains fascinating background information and provides easy
to follow step-by-step instructions and illustrations to help you
create your own powerful objects of intention.
176 page paperback with over 100 colour photographs.*

978-1-84409-161-4

Practical Conscious Creation
by Jackie Lapin

Exploring the principles of Conscious Creation – a methodology for re-energizing and re-empowering one's daily experiences – this overview provides all the necessary tools for creating the life one desires. It demonstrates how to employ this powerful form of inspired thought in all actions, decisions, and routines. Filled with specific and imaginative practices, it teaches how to use the Law of Attraction with Conscious Visualization in order to proactively choose one's future, rather than merely passively waiting for something to happen. 256 page paperback with 15 line drawings

978-1-84409-561-2

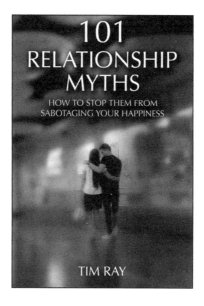

101 Relationship Myths
by Tim Ray

*The book's basic premise is that most of us believe in a wide range
of myths about men and women, love and relationships that we
have never questioned. It is our continuing belief in these myths
that confuses us and makes us unhappy in our relationships.
To help readers understand the power these beliefs hold in our lives,
Tim identifies some of our most common "relationship myths". And
then he shows us how we can free ourselves from them. The result is
much greater clarity, joy and love in our relationships.*
192 pages paperback

978-1-84409-584-1

FINDHORN PRESS

Life-Changing Books

For a complete catalogue,
please contact:

Findhorn Press Ltd
117-121 High Street,
Forres IV36 1AB,
Scotland, UK

t +44 (0)1309 690582
f +44 (0)131 777 2711
e info@findhornpress.com

or consult our catalogue online
(with secure order facility) on
www.findhornpress.com

For information on the Findhorn Foundation:
www.findhorn.org